WHAT LIES BENEATH

WHAT LIES BENEATH

A MEMOIR

by

ELSPETH SANDYS

OTAGO

For Roy and Jeanette Walker

First published 2014
Copyright © Elspeth Sandys

Publisher: Rachel Scott
Editor: Rachel Scott
Design/layout: Fiona Moffat

Printed in New Zealand by Wickliffe New Zealand Ltd

Front cover: Elspeth's father, Tom Somerville, carried this little photo of his daughter in his wallet until the day he died.

This is a true story, based on the events of my early life. However, for obvious reasons, some parts have had to be imagined. Where such passages occur I have endeavoured to stay within the facts as I understand them. But facts are slippery things, especially where alternative versions of events exist. Like Michael Ondaatje in his brilliant memoir *Running in the Family*, which he describes as 'not a history but a portrait', I have chosen the versions that *feel* true.

Acknowledgements

Grateful thanks are due to Sir James Wallace, and the University of Otago Wallace Residency at The Pah Homestead, which he established, and which I was lucky enough to be awarded in 2012. Without this support, and the gift of time to write, I may never have started the memoir.

I am indebted to my half-sister, Gilda, the first to welcome me into the Tompkins family. Not only did she facilitate introductions to others in the family, but she generously shared what information she had about the past.

Thanks also to Sir David Tompkins, Judith Doyle and Dr Jocelyn Harris, who read the manuscript and were most generous in their support and advice.

'So we beat on, boats against the current,
borne back ceaselessly into the past.'
SCOTT FITZGERALD, *THE GREAT GATSBY*

PART ONE: BEFORE

'All sorrows can be borne if you put them in a story,
or tell a story about them.'
ISAK DINESEN

Chapter One

'The desires of the heart are as crooked as corkscrews,
Not to be born is the best for man ...'
W.H. Auden

New Plymouth, New Zealand, June 1939

The phone rings in my father's house. A winter evening made colder by the talk, on the wireless, of war.

My father steps out of the warm sitting room into the draughty hallway. Instinctively he glances up the stairs, wondering if the phone, which rings rarely, has woken his two sleeping children. Satisfied all is well, and his evening not about to be interrupted by fractious toddlers, he picks up the receiver. 'Ken Tompkins,' he says.

The voice on the other end of the line is familiar: Arnie Traherne, a fellow Mason. He gets straight to the point. The days of party lines, when conversations could be listened in to by curious neighbours, may be over, but that's no excuse for wasting time in idle chat. 'I understand you know Betty James,' Arnie says.

My father lets out a small involuntary gasp. 'Good heavens,' he says. 'Betty James. Years since … Family had a bach near ours at Raglan. Must be in her late twenties by now. Last I heard she was working in Wellington.'

'Well, she's heading this way. Not sure what the story is.'

'Her brother's still in New Plymouth, isn't he? One of her brothers. Lives in the old family home.'

'Donald. Accountant at Tate and Brumby.'

'Never could tell those James boys apart.'

'You're right about Wellington. She's been working as a secretary to some chap in Cabinet. Jones, Minister of Defence, was what my wife heard.'

'Done well for herself then.'

'Would seem so.'

'So what exactly is the trouble? I'd have thought she'd be married by now.'

'Donald wasn't very forthcoming.'

'Well, those James boys were a Bolshie lot as I remember.'

'I only know the family by name. But the wife and Betty were at school together. That's why I'm ringing. Vera thought you and Olive might, you know, rally round. Of course we'll do our bit too.'

'And you've no idea …?'

'All her brother would say was that she's in a bit of a spot. Vera thinks there's probably a chap in it somewhere.'

My father glances at himself in the hall mirror. He sees a man in his mid-thirties, with a good head of almost blond hair, clean-shaven cheeks and chin, and piercing blue eyes that every girl he has known, with the exception of his unimpressed sisters, has remarked on. 'You know who you look like, don't you?' the girl whose reputation he was supposed to have ruined at varsity said to him the day they met. 'Scott Fitzgerald.' My father grins. Those were the days …

'I did hear something about an engagement,' he says into the phone.

'Then I expect that's at the bottom of it.'

My father smoothes his hand over his hair. Who would I rather look like? he asks the mirror. A drunken Yankee novelist, or what I am, a successful dental surgeon, with a beautiful wife, two children under five and a third on the way?

He turns his head, struck suddenly by the image of a leggy teenager, five years younger than he is, peering at him over the shoulder of one of her brothers. The Tompkins family has been sharing the beach at Raglan with the James clan every summer for as far back as he can remember. At nineteen, a year into his studies at the Otago Dental School, spending the best part of a month with his parents and older married siblings and their noisy offspring was not his idea of a good time. But that was before he spotted Betty James. It hadn't been easy separating her from her posse of brothers, but he'd managed it. A walk along the beach, followed by a detour into the sandhills, soon got him what he wanted. It was, as he explained to the brother (Donald?) who caught them kissing, only a bit of fun. 'Fun!' the lout had shouted. 'She's fourteen years old!'

'I'll do what I can,' my father promises. 'Though with all this talk of war …' He doesn't bother to finish the sentence. What he's thinking is, I won't worry Olive with this. The name 'James' has lost whatever cachet it once had in New Plymouth. It's possible Olive's never even heard of the family. The bach at Raglan was sold long before Olive came on the scene.

'Who was that?' my father's wife asks when he returns to the sitting room. The wireless, with its distressing predictions, has been switched off. The only sound in the room, apart from the loudly ticking clock on the mantelpiece, is the rhythmic staccato of Olive's knitting needles.

'Just some Masons' business,' my father answers. 'Nothing for you to worry about.'

Chapter Two

....

'Nothing happens without consequences;
nothing ever did happen without antecedents.'
ANON

Wellington, June 1939

My mother stands on the platform of the Wellington Railway Station, wrapped in a fur coat, her father's battered suitcase on the ground beside her, her gloved hands plunged into the sleeves of her coat. It's 8.27 am. She should be at work. She's never missed a day before.

'Betty James, what would I do without you?' Her boss's voice tolls like a school bell in her head.

'You'll have to do without me when I'm married, Minister.' First time she said those words, flashing the tiny diamond on her left hand, they both laughed. But as a year passed, then another, and another, the joke wore thin.

My mother throws back her head. Strange animal whimperings keep escaping from her lips. She tries to force the sounds back, but they seem to have a life of their own. So she stands at a distance from the other travellers, her back turned on the waiting train as if the journey to come were a matter of complete indifference to her.

The noise of the engine, building up steam, is deafening. Any minute now the doors will open, and the passengers waiting on the platform will surge forward like eager puppies scenting food. Someone sneezes. A mother calls out to a child. A man laughs. Above their heads, puffs of smoke cling, like pale bats, to the station roof.

'Can I come home?' she'd sobbed down the phone to her brother last night.

'What about your job?' Donald had asked.

'*Please*, Donald ...'

Her brother's hesitation had lasted just long enough for Betty to feel panic rising. Like everyone else in the family, Donald had got used to Gavin being around. 'Isn't it time you two got hitched?' he was always teasing. 'This is turning out to be the longest engagement in history.'

'You can have your old room back,' Donald said. 'Kids can double up.'

A loud voice announces the imminent departure of the train for New Plymouth. My mother picks up her case, joins the knots of people huddled around the now open doors.

Six hours later she is back in her childhood home.

*****

My father stands at the door of a large wooden house in the old part of town. The house, he observes smugly – the Jameses, with their connections to the first ships to arrive in New Plymouth from England, considered themselves above everyone else – is badly in need of a coat of paint. 'Ken Tompkins,' he says, to the woman who opens the door. 'I telephoned earlier.'

'You've come to see Betty,' the woman says.

My father nods. So this is Donald's wife, he's thinking. Not much of a looker. But then neither is Donald. Betty was the one with the looks in that family.

The woman wipes her hands on her apron. Thin streaks of red jam appear like wounds across her stomach. 'You better come in,' she says.

My father is led into a large, dimly lit room, smelling strongly of furniture wax. It wouldn't have surprised him to see white covers over the furniture – chairs, sideboard, glass cabinet, matching settees. The room reeks of preservation. The only pictures hanging on the wall are a coloured portrait of the new King and Queen, and Donald's wedding photo. A grinning Betty, in flower-girl pink, leaps out at him.

Left alone, my father is seized by misgivings. What is he doing here? It's not as if he's a friend, not really. Apart from those summer weeks at Raglan the families had little or nothing to do with each other. The Tompkinses lived in the Waikato, the Jameses in Taranaki. The fact that he chose to live and work in New Plymouth had nothing to do with those all but forgotten summer holidays.

Donald's wife has gone to fetch her husband. She didn't say anything about Betty. Which means he's wasting his time, so he'll make his excuses and head home. Olive has been complaining of tiredness. To be expected, with two active toddlers and a baby on the way, but it's out of character for her to complain. If he leaves now he'll be in time to help put the children to bed.

The door opens. Donald, my uncle, enters the room. Donald doesn't like my father. Never has. What he remembers of those Raglan summers is how much more fun the older Tompkins siblings were than their spoiled youngest brother. 'You've come to enquire after Betty,' he says, holding out his hand.

My father nods. Smiling doesn't seem appropriate, given the circumstances, not that he knows yet what those circumstances are. 'My wife sends her greetings. She's not well, which is why I'm here.'

My uncle indicates the settees. He waits for my father to sit, then sits opposite him. 'Sorry to hear about Mrs Tompkins,' he says. 'Hope she'll be better soon.'

'You know how it is with a young family.'

'I've two myself. You probably heard them as you came in.'

'So how *is* Betty?' my father says. 'I understand she's had a bit of a setback.'

Uncle Donald doesn't answer immediately. He frowns, looks up at the ceiling, bites the top of his thumb, then frowns again. 'Broken engagement,' he reveals. 'Wouldn't matter so much if it hadn't been such a long haul. Seven years come Christmas.'

'I see.'

'Can't get much out of her. The swine broke it off in a letter, that's all I know. Cowardly way to go about things in my opinion.'

'Sounds as if your sister might be better off without him.'

'And to think I took him for a decent joker … Just goes to show.'

My father feels for his packet of cigarettes. No sign of ashtrays in the room. And no sign of a fire being lit or a heater turned on. 'Do you mind?' he asks, holding up his packet of Craven A.

My uncle shrugs.

'Do you still call yourselves Hilton James?' my father can't resist asking. He remembers teasing Betty about that the day he lured her into the sand hills. 'You make it sound like we're snobs,' she'd answered hotly. 'It's a middle name, that's all.'

'Which you all use,' he'd pointed out. 'And what's wrong with that?' He'd liked it that she was edgy with him. Made him feel they were on an equal footing.

My father peers at my uncle through a screen of smoke. Either he hasn't heard the question, or he's decided not to answer. Is this the brother who caught him kissing Betty? If it is, it would explain the extra chill in the air. He draws more smoke into his lungs, savouring the fleeting warmth it provides. 'Look,' he says, 'my wife instructed me to do whatever I could. She never knew Betty but she remembers the family and, well, she has a kind heart … Sometimes in these situations it's easier to talk to an outsider …' When there's no response he adds, for good measure, 'Sooner your sister sees this fellow who's jilted her for what he really is, the better. What was he doing expecting her to wait so long anyway?'

'Saving for a house,' my uncle informs him.

My father shakes his head. After all I *can* see Betty in you, he's thinking: same unruly dark hair, though I don't imagine Betty's is thinning on the top as yours is; same wide mouth; same tendency to tower over people. Even as a teenager Betty was tall, with strong limbs. A tomboy was what she was, and a damned attractive one at that.

'Well, I won't keep you,' he says, stubbing out his cigarette. 'Perhaps you'd tell your sister I called. And give her my best.'

It might have ended there, in which case I would not be writing this. But as my father is being shepherded out the door Betty appears at the end of the corridor. There's only the faint wash of light from the room they've just left to illuminate the passageway, so my father has to squint to see the figure hovering uncertainly in the semi-darkness. 'Hello there,' he says.

Nothing happens for a second or two, then Betty starts to walk towards him. 'Ken Tompkins,' she says. 'What a surprise.'

'I've come to see how you are,' my father answers. He wouldn't have recognised her. Not that she looks ill. Pale, and in need of sleep, sure, but with her luscious curls limp around her shoulders, and her luminous brown eyes concealed behind a raised hand, there's nothing to remind him of the cheeky teenager he'd been so keen to kiss. 'Hiding away from your friends,' he scolds. 'What sort of carry-on is that?'

My mother frowns. *Friends*, she's thinking. I wasn't aware we were friends.

'You know what you need,' my father says briskly, holding out his hand to her. 'You need to be taken out of yourself. Moping about in the dark won't solve anything.' She takes his hand, but only for a second, sliding hers out before he has time to give it an encouraging squeeze. 'Look,' he says, aware of Donald hovering behind him, 'I have to make a home visit up-country on Saturday. What say I take you with me? I seem to remember you were keen on driving. Always pestering my older brother to take you for a spin. Used to make me quite jealous. So what do you say? A drive into the country, back in time for tea … Come on, Betty, say yes. It'll do you good.'

My mother spreads the fingers of her left hand. All that remains of her engagement is the high-water mark on her ring finger. Is this the trigger? Or have my father's words spun a web from which she has, at this moment, no wish to escape? All she'd wanted was to be back in her old home, sleeping in her old bed, but after two days she feels trapped. Donald's wife is kind, but the way she looks at her, eyes full of pity, sets my mother's teeth on edge. One of the many lessons of her childhood, being raised among a cabal of brothers, was that it was better to be hated than pitied. She shouldn't have come, that's the truth of the matter. Her other brothers, if they were here, would tell her a broken heart is a puny affair, not worth all the fuss she's making. Donald has already told her she's better off without a man who could make her wait seven years. What he'd meant of course was that Gavin couldn't have been in love with her the way a man should be in love with a woman. Was that true? Their times alone had been fond enough, but he'd never seemed to have any trouble stopping before things got out of hand. Was that her fault? Perhaps she should have encouraged him. Perhaps he thought she was cold. How was she to know? All she knew was that people were pitying her, and she couldn't stand it.

'Thank you,' she says, relieved to see there is not an ounce of pity in Ken Tompkins' blue eyes. 'A drive would be nice.'

Chapter Three

'Time is not a line but a dimension,
like the dimensions of space.'
MARGARET ATWOOD

Two days later my mother takes the train back to Wellington. 'I'm fine, truly,' she assured her brother. 'It's kind of you and Laurel to say I can stay longer, but I'm all right now … Sorry I made such a fuss.'

My father's 'home visit', the ostensible reason for the drive into the country, had been cancelled at the last minute. 'Are you sure?' my mother had said to him, when he insisted on taking her for a drive anyway. 'Can you spare the time?'

'I don't usually work weekends,' he'd answered. 'Unless there's an emergency.'

'What about your family?'

'It's their day with the in-laws.'

'Well, if you're sure,' my mother had said.

Now she's back in Wellington, a wet, windy Sunday evening, walking from the train station to the cable-car halfway up Lambton Quay. The animal whimperings have stopped. Outwardly calm, she crosses the road to avoid walking past the tearoom where she and Gavin used to meet. His letter gave no reason for the break-up. Just said how sorry he was, and wished her well.

The street is almost empty. The few people who do hurry past her look as anxious as she is to reach safe haven. A woman struggles with an umbrella that the wind has turned inside out. A man eyes her furtively from under his hat. Lights swim in the damp patches on the road.

As the cable-car makes its slow way up the hill, my mother plans what she will say to her boss tomorrow morning when she turns up for work. She won't, of course, mention Gavin. And if she's asked about the absence of the ring on her finger, she'll say she lost it.

Her home is a flat on Upland Road which she shares with Violet, a stenographer in a legal office. They are good, though not especially close, friends. Vi will be pleased to see her back so soon. She doesn't like being in the flat on her own. They'll eat toast and drink hot chocolate, and Vi, who knows about Gavin, will ask her how she is, and she'll insist she's fine, 'better off without him'. She'll say nothing about the drive in the country, though. That will remain her secret. But at least she knows now that she's not cold. And when she falls asleep it will not be Gavin's cool grey eyes she sees, but eyes so blue they make her think of icebergs.

*****

'Glad to have you back,' the Minister says as my mother walks through the door. To her relief he doesn't mention her absence. She was going to say she'd had a touch of the flu that's been going around – the blotchy patches on her cheeks and red rims around her eyes should confirm her story – but there's no need. 'If there's going to be a war,' her boss says, looking at her with a mixture of sternness and curiosity, 'and I don't think "if" comes into it, I'm going to need you here round the clock.'

*****

Over the next few hectic weeks Betty works as if she alone can hold back the horror that is coming. A constant stream of messages passes between her Minister's office and the Prime Minister's. Telegrams and phone calls interrupt the daily business of filing and typing. She tries not to think about Gavin, and succeeds, some days, for as much as ten minutes at a time. When she thinks about the drive into the country it's as if it happened to someone else. She remembers it the way you remember a film, or a dream. When, as happens often now, she feels nauseous, she puts it down to the shock she has suffered, and the anxiety everyone is feeling as Europe inches towards war.

*****

Early in August my mother visits a doctor – not her usual one but a name chosen at random in a part of the city far from where she lives. Her sickness has persisted; it can no longer be explained away by events on the other side of the world. When the doctor tells her she is pregnant, she faints. The doctor, guessing there is no husband, is kind. He asks about her family; talks to her about adoption; gives her the name of an organisation founded to help young women in her position.

For the rest of the day she wanders the chilly streets in a daze. She takes the cable-car to the top of the hill, but instead of going home she plunges into the upper reaches of the Botanic Gardens. Normally alert to the changes in the seasons, she ignores the snowdrops hiding shyly among the long grasses, and sets her face into the wind, hoping if she walks fast enough and far enough, by the end of the day there will be nothing left of her shame. The few other people out braving the wintry wind glance at her as she stumbles past but she doesn't see them.

It's dark by the time she returns to the flat. The sound of her key in the door adds another dimension to her pain. She's a prisoner now, with no hope of escape.

'What's happened?' Vi says, jumping up from the sofa the moment Betty appears in the sitting room. 'You look as if you've seen a ghost.'

Betty shakes her head. She can't even begin to say the words.

'Here, sit down.' Vi half pushes half pulls Betty onto the sofa. 'Tea. There's still some in the pot. You can tell me what's happened over a cup of tea.'

At first Betty denies it's anything other than the old trouble – a broken heart, the broken world – but Vi persists, and the truth comes out.

'Oh God,' Vi says, instinctively lowering her voice. 'Oh dearie dearie me. What are you going to do? … You're sure …? You … Who was it? Was it …?' She mouths the word 'Gavin'.

Betty shakes her head.

'Who then?'

'Does it matter?'

'Of course it matters. He must marry you. He has to marry you.'

Betty shakes her head again, angrily this time.

'He seduced you, didn't he, this man. I know you, Betty. This is not you. You're not the sort of girl who …'

Betty laughs. It's a depressing sound. 'Hardly a girl,' she protests. 'Thirty next birthday.'

'That's still young.'

'He can't marry me, Vi. He's married already.'

Vi's mouth opens, then shuts again. There are no words for this situation. This kind of thing happens to other people, not to people she knows.

'He has children,' Betty adds. 'His wife is pregnant.'

Vi balls up her fists and presses them into her eyes. 'On second thoughts don't tell me his name,' she mutters. 'If I know who he is I might …'

'He was kind, he listened. It was a relief to talk … And he made me laugh. I can't tell you how good that felt …'

'He seduced you.'

'It only happened once. I thought, as I'd never … as I was still … Obviously I was wrong.'

It's nearly midnight when Vi finally insists they stop talking and go to bed. Whatever lies ahead they still have to go to work in the morning. They've gone over and over the same few facts, as if by repeating the words they can change the reality.

*****

But one thing *has* changed. Betty has conceded the need to write to the father of her child. 'Though I still don't see what he can do,' she'd protested, frowning fiercely, every muscle in her face working to keep tears at bay.

'He can give you money,' Vi had replied.

'For what? I'm not going to get rid … if that's what you're thinking. I couldn't.'

'Of course not. That would be … But you'll need money. You'll have to stop work at some point. Then what?'

And so a plan of sorts emerged. Betty will have the baby in a town where nobody knows her, where she can pass herself off as a widow. 'Perhaps this war everyone's talking about will work in my favour,' she'd said, in a forlorn attempt to lighten the mood. 'I can pretend I'm a war widow.'

'Only difference is, you won't have a widow's pension,' Vi had pointed out. 'In fact, unless your family's prepared to help, you won't have any money at all.'

It's that word *family* that echoes in Betty's mind as she drifts in and out of sleep. Brothers, uncles, aunts, cousins – what will they say, what will they think? In the space of one afternoon everything in her life has changed. It would help if she could say she couldn't remember, that it had all been a dream, but since the visit to the doctor the opposite has been true. Every moment of that long afternoon has returned to haunt her. I'm not Betty, she kept saying to herself, as Ken's hands surged through her layers of clothing, undoing, loosening, probing … I'm no one. I don't have a name …

Chapter Four

....

'At last the secret is out, as it always must come in the end,
The delicious story is ripe to tell to the intimate friend ...'
W.H. AUDEN

Dear Betty,

Your letter is very shocking. Frankly I find it hard to believe. Are
you completely sure? You were in quite a state as I recall, though
perfectly clear, as I also recall, that what we did was all right with
you. I'm sorry you're feeling as you are, but until I can be sure this is
not some hysterical manifestation, I feel disinclined to say more.

Ken

PS. I trust there will be no further need for communication, but if
there is, would you kindly address correspondence to the surgery
and not to the house ...'

My father takes care addressing and sealing the envelope. He has to be sure it will reach its destination. 'MISS BETTY HILTON JAMES' he writes in bold letters. He's toyed with the idea of sending it to her work address, but Upland Road will do, for now. If there's any further correspondence he'll write to her care of the Ministry of Defence. Betty is a grown woman. She knew what she was doing. So what if she was a virgin? She'd made it abundantly clear she wished that to change. He has nothing to reproach himself with.

*****

Dear Sis,

Your letter came as a shock, but not as much of a shock I dare say as the one you got when you were told of your condition. I'll say nothing of my own feelings in this matter. Or of Laurel's. We are your family and we will support you in any way we can.

You have chosen to protect the blackguard who did this to you. I take it that means it is not Gavin. But if you think this man, whoever he is – and I suspect it's someone not a million miles from our front door – can escape his responsibilities, you are mistaken. He has to answer for his actions.

You have asked me not to reveal the facts to the rest of the family. I will honour that for now, but I don't see how you can hope to hide your condition indefinitely. Unless of course you decide on a more drastic course of action.

I wish I could offer material help but as you know this house is mortgaged to the hilt. But it is your home, the place where we were all brought up, and the door will always be open for you.

Your loving brother,

Don

*****

The days following the receipt of these two letters are outwardly no different from any other day of my mother's working life. Each morning she hurries along Upland Road to the cable-car terminus, clinging to the strap as the crowded car hurtles down the hill, fighting the waves of nausea that, on bad days, force her to push through the crush of bodies exiting the car to hurl herself and the contents of her stomach into the gutter. She works diligently, making no complaint when the worsening international situation keeps her tied to her desk till long after dark. If she is quieter than usual no one comments. With the sense of dread as palpable in the streets of Wellington as the coughs and sniffles of winter colds and flu, the only people raising their voices are street-corner orators, and newspaper boys shouting the latest headlines. It's barely twenty years since the last 'war to end all wars'. Many of the people huddled nervously around wireless sets, and hunched over newspapers in tearooms and bars, experienced the horror of that conflict first hand. Those who didn't, know the statistics – New Zealand lost more men, per capita, than any other country in the world. How can it be happening again?

The nights are worse. Betty knows the outward continuity of her life is a lie, and soon, whether war breaks out or not, everything will change. As she lies awake in her narrow bed, her restless mind jumps from images of the new life she wants so desperately to believe in, a life in which she is a mother to her child, to nightmare scenes where she is hauled screaming out onto the street, to be shamed in front of her family and friends. When she thinks of my father it's as if a splinter has lodged in her eye, and all her efforts to dislodge it only bury it deeper. When she thinks of Gavin her mouth goes dry and she has to force the air out of her rebelling lungs. No one will want her now. She is soiled goods.

*****

Towards the end of August my mother writes a second letter to my father. Violet has persuaded her she must ask for his financial help. 'He can't go on pretending it hasn't happened,' she said.

Her brother, making no attempt to hide his disgust, has said the same.

But it's not easy to find the right words. She's never asked anyone for money before. The thought of what Ken might write in reply sends her racing to the bathroom.

> *Dear Ken,*
>
> *I am now eight weeks pregnant. There is no doubt. I intend to keep the baby. Please let me know what you are prepared to do for me and the child. I promise to keep your identity secret.*
>
> *Betty*

*****

Opening the letter in his surgery my father, who considers swearing a sign of poor breeding, lets out an involuntary curse. That one small fall from grace should lead to *this* is not just a cruel joke on God's part, it's a sick one. It's not as if it was even a particularly satisfactory encounter, at least not from his point of view. 'Damn and blast the woman!' he says, screwing the letter up into a tight ball. He'd had a couple of scares like this at varsity, but luckily they turned out to be false alarms. He's still not convinced this won't go the same way. Extracting money from a man gullible enough to believe he's about to become a father is one of the oldest tricks in the business. 'Damn and blast!' he says again. He's not a student any more. He's a married man, with a family and a reputation to protect.

He glances at his watch. His nurse is not due in till ten. He has time to write a note, enclosing a cheque for a hundred pounds. Hopefully that will keep Betty quiet. He should have sent money at the start. She might have got rid of the problem then, if indeed there is a problem. Madness to think she can keep the baby. What sort of life would she be condemning the child to? Her only course is to put it up for adoption. A hundred pounds should more than cover that.

*****

On the evening of 3 September Michael Joseph Savage, Prime Minister of New Zealand, informs his fellow citizens that the country is at war. 'Where Britain goes we go,' he declares. 'Where she stands we stand.'

My mother, alerted in advance to the situation, stands by the office wireless, her arms wrapped tightly around her stomach, her shallow breathing audible in the hushed room. 'You best get off home,' the Minister says when the announcement comes to an end. 'I'm going to need you here first thing.'

As she makes her way to the cable-car she finds herself wishing for a desperate moment that the war would come to New Zealand, and a bomb fall on her as she walks. Everywhere she looks she sees faces etched with anxiety. Spring has come to the city, but its mood is lost on the resigned citizens of this, the most southern of the Empire's capitals. The gung-ho emotions that sent thousands of young Kiwis to their deaths at Gallipoli, and in the trenches of France and Belgium, are conspicuously absent. New Zealand, recognising the threat Nazism poses, will go to war, but this time it will go with a heavy heart.

How long can I live on a hundred pounds? my mother asks herself as she waits for the up car to arrive. How long can I go on concealing my changing shape?

Chapter Five

....

'The past is unpredictable.'
RUSSIAN SAYING

A few days after the receipt of my father's cheque, my mother receives a letter from a school friend in New Plymouth. 'Absolutely nothing changes in this town,' Jean writes. 'People die, people get born, and that's about it. You'd never know there was a war on ... You've probably heard that Olive Tompkins has had another baby, a girl. That makes three under five. I wonder if the poor woman knew she was marrying a compulsive breeder. Deidre Marshall – remember her? – told me Olive wasn't well. Probably that thing women get after having a baby, post something or other ...'

My mother runs out of the flat, on to the street. It's a Saturday morning. Men congregate around the entrance to the Gardens, discussing the war, and the likely outcome of the 2 pm race at Ellerslie. She pushes past them, deaf to the man who whistles at her, hearing only the voices in her head. 'Look, it's Betty James. Yes, she's pregnant. Shocking, isn't it? No one knows who the father is.' She doesn't stop till she reaches the bench at the back of the rose garden. Shaded by a tall pohutukawa, this bench is her sanctuary. She has spent more hours hiding from the world on its mossy seat than she has in her bed.

'A girl,' she murmurs. 'A daughter ...' She places a hand over her stomach, as if to shield the child growing inside her from the awful truth of its parentage. There will be rejoicing in the Tompkins home, despite Olive not being well. Friends will come calling bearing gifts. The two older children will run in and out of the nursery like excited rabbits. 'Let me hold her, let me ...' Ken will look on with pride: pride in his children; in his beautiful wife; in the respect he has earned for his pioneering dental methods. 'Prevention, that's the key,' he'd told her, as the town dwindled into nothing behind them and there was only the dull tapestry of paddocks dotted with black and white cows to distract her from her misery. The mountain, whose changing moods had so often, in the past, kept pace with her own, was shrouded in mist. 'With fluoride in the water, and a daily programme of oral hygiene, filling children's teeth with amalgam should become a thing of the past.' How certain he'd been, not just of himself and his work, but that everything would be all right. 'Think of it as something that was bound to happen,' he said when it was over. 'If not with me then with someone else. And don't worry. You'll be right as rain.'

But I'm not, am I, she answers him now. I'll never be right as rain again.

Chapter Six

·······································

'History makes sense of memory.
It is a grid for individual experience.'
LISA APPIGNANESI

Over the next two months the papers are filled not so much with what is happening as with what is not happening. One paper, quoting Winston Churchill, refers to it as 'The Twilight War'. Another, quoting the *Washington Post*, calls it 'The Phoney War'. There's fighting in Poland but almost nowhere else. The British response to the presence of enemy troops along the Siegfried Line is to bomb Germany with propaganda pamphlets. 'What on earth do they think they're doing?' Betty's boss exclaims, shaking his head in disbelief. 'They might just as well drop a year's supply of toilet paper. That's what those pamphlets will be used for.'

But when my mother, realising she can't leave it any longer, tells him she is resigning, he is silent. For a few paralysing seconds she thinks he must have guessed the reason for her resignation. Why else would his face have turned to stone? Then he says, the bitter words dropping like poison into her ears, 'So you want to see yourself in uniform, do you? Office life not exciting enough for you?'

She tries to protest, but he cuts her short. 'Spare me the explanation,' he snaps. 'It's still a free country. You can do whatever you want.'

*****

The week of my mother's resignation is an especially satisfying one for my father. An envelope with the seal of the New Zealand Dental Association arrives in the post for him. His wife is curious. What are they writing to you about, she wants to know? He's curious himself, but for the time being the letter must wait. If it's what he thinks it is, the matter will need careful handling. 'What's for tea?' he asks, wrinkling his nose. The smell coming from the oven reminds him how hungry he is.

'Steak and kidney pie … Aren't you going to open it?' Olive asks, as he stows the letter in his back pocket.

'What's the betting it's yet another appeal for money? "Distressed Dental Folk", something of that ilk.' He moves close to his wife and nuzzles her in the neck. 'I'm hungry as a horse,' he murmurs.

Olive laughs. 'Stop nibbling me then, and I'll dish up.'

With tea over, and the children settled for the night, my father tells his wife he'll join her shortly in the sitting room. 'A bit of paperwork to attend to,' he explains, with at least some truth.

Reaching the sanctity of his den, he takes the envelope out of his pocket and weighs it in his hand. Of course it might be nothing at all, he says to himself. If not an appeal for money, then a response to the article he published recently in the quarterly journal. Not everyone agrees with him about the value of adding fluoride to the water supply. There's bound to be correspondence. But as he slides a fingernail under the flap he knows instinctively that it's neither of these things. Its what he's been waiting for, the answer to his application for a fellowship to join the team presently researching fluoridation in Washington. 'It is my great pleasure to inform you … A three-month visa has been arranged … Your passage has been booked on the SS *Aramoana*, sailing from Auckland on December 27th …'

'I only didn't tell you because I didn't want you to worry,' he insists when he's broken the news to his wife. He's back in the sitting room. The wireless is on – the dance music they both like – but neither of them is listening. The way Olive is looking at him is making him feel decidedly uncomfortable. When did she get those shadows under her eyes? And why, despite the rouge on her cheeks, does she look so pale?

'Oh, so that makes it all right, does it?' Olive answers him. 'I wasn't to worry while you were waiting to hear, but it's all right for me to worry now.'

'If it's the war you're worrying about …'

'Actually, Ken, it's not. Though no doubt it will be by the time you go. Because you are going, aren't you? Nothing I say will make the slightest difference.'

He doesn't have an answer for that, so he busies himself lighting a cigarette and waits for the inquisition to end.

'When?' Olive says. 'When did you apply for this thing?'

'Does that matter?'

'Tell me, please.'

'Let me think … Sometime in September must have been. Why?'

He sees at once how badly he's blundered. 'After my visit to Doctor Land,' Olive says.

Ken swears under his breath. Land was an old fool, putting the wind up his wife when all that was wrong with her was exhaustion. ('I'm not happy about her colour,' he'd said when Olive was out of hearing. 'Or her blood pressure. I'd like to run some tests.') 'Must have been August,' he corrects himself now. 'It certainly wasn't after …'

'And why exactly did you apply? And please don't say to "keep abreast". There are other ways to do that.'

'I know,' he admits humbly. 'And I'm sorry, truly sorry. At the time …' (At the time it was another woman and another birth I wanted to get away from, is what he's thinking. Never for a moment have I wanted to get away from you.) '"Peace in our time",' he says. 'I believed it. Simple as that.'

'Instead of which we are at war,' Olive says. 'And Dr Land still doesn't know what's wrong with me.'

*****

Olive was right about my father's determination to go to Washington. His arguments, presented one after the other, might not have swayed a more determined adversary, but it was not in Olive's nature to put up a fight.

'It would be a betrayal to back down now,' he points out, 'after the board have put their faith in me. Three months will pass in a flash. Especially with a Karitane nurse coming in every day to help … No no no,' he insists, when Olive protests at the cost of such an arrangement, 'I've made up my mind. You're to have help, and that's an end to it. I feel badly enough leaving you with the children. At least this way I know you won't be alone …'

As for the travel side of things, he jokes that with the war confined to Poland, crossing the ocean will be no more dangerous than crossing the road. Surely she can see how important this trip is? New Zealand has one of the worst dental records in the developed world. Something has to explain that. What's the point of teaching people how to look after their teeth if the water they drink is the cause of the problem?

*****

Meanwhile my mother has moved in with her brother. With no money coming in she couldn't stay on in the Upland Road flat. Donald has offered her a home for as long as she needs it.

It's the second week in January. Uncle Donald's children – my first cousins – are playing in the back garden. My aunt is in the kitchen, one eye on the children, the other on the vegetables simmering on the range. The front door slams. My aunt smiles – her husband is home early tonight.

'How's my favourite girl?' Donald says, circling his wife's waist from behind, kissing the tiny pool of sweat that has gathered behind her ear. 'Betty in her room?'

Laurel lifts her head and smiles into her husband's eyes. 'I tried to get her to sit in the garden,' she says. 'No one would see her there. Well, only Mrs B, and she's half blind.'

'Hmm …' Donald lifts a lid from one of the saucepans; replaces it with a clang. 'I never thought I'd wish summer away, but this one …'

Later, seated around the wireless in the sitting room, Donald, at a sign from Laurel, directs an apparently casual remark to his sister. This is no accident, but part of a plan hatched by husband and wife between putting the children to bed and retiring with their Ovaltine to listen to the 9 o'clock news. Three weeks ago the First NZ Echelon sailed to North Africa. Despite the false sense of security generated by the 'phoney war', there is tension in the country as people wait to hear news of where the Kiwi soldiers are to be deployed. But the tension in my uncle's sitting room on that warm summer evening has nothing to do with the war. Betty's refusal to name the father of her child has only fuelled speculation (her pregnancy is no longer a secret in the family) about the identity of her seducer. Right from the beginning Donald and his wife have had their suspicions, but it's only today, with its unexpected development, that an opportunity has arisen to settle the matter.

'Guess who I bumped into this morning,' Donald says.

Betty, hunched over her sewing, answers him with a small shrug.

'Lance Tompkins. You used to rather like him, as I remember.'

Betty looks up. So far she has made five baby gowns, each one exquisitely hemstitched, with satin ribbons at the neck and tiny blue and yellow flowers embroidered across the chest. This one is to be the last. Her needle, poised in mid-air, glints in the light from the standing lamp by her chair.

'He's a lawyer,' Donald goes on. 'Well, you probably know that. Has a practice in Hamilton. It was good to see him again. I always liked Lance.'

Betty lowers her arm. The needle anchors itself in a half-finished flower.

'He had some interesting news about Ken,' Donald says, leaning forward to catch the light. The nights are starting to draw in. What's left of the daylight lingers in the room, as if unsure of its welcome. 'He's in Washington. That's Washington, America. Sailed just after Christmas apparently.'

'*What?*'

Donald exchanges a glance with his wife. He's used to the way his sister looks these days – the dark rings under her eyes; the telltale blotches on her cheeks – but the expression on her face now is new. Had he leapt up and slapped her she could not have looked more stunned.

'What did you just say?'

'He was awarded a scholarship of some kind. He'll be away three months.'

Betty's head drops into her hands. Donald, catching his wife's eye, nods. The answer to their question is there in front of them. 'It's him, isn't it?' he says quietly. 'I thought so … Bastard!'

Laurel gets up from her chair and kneels by Betty's side. 'He does know, does he, dear?' she asks. 'You have told him?'

Betty nods.

'And what was his reaction?'

'He sent me a hundred pounds.'

Donald smashes his fists down on the arms of his chair. 'Right! That's it,' he says, jumping to his feet. 'A miserly one hundred pounds in return for ruining your life.'

'Where are you going?' Laurel asks.

'Where do you think?'

'But he's not there. He's in Washington.'

'His wife's there.'

'Donald, no! You mustn't drag Olive into this. It's not her fault.'

My uncle comes to a halt in the middle of the room. He doesn't know what to do with his anger. The only fighting he's ever known is childhood rough and tumble, but if Ken Tompkins were to walk through that door now he would fall on him like a wild animal. What kind of man flees the country leaving his wife and his – he silently chokes on the word – *mistress*, to clean up the mess he's created?

'I think the person you should be talking to is Lance,' Laurel says, moving to stand by her husband, her eyes appealing to him to stay calm. 'You said he was going to be in town for a few days …'

'Lance? What's it got to do with him?'

'He's a lawyer, isn't he?'

Donald shakes his head, not in denial but in an attempt to obliterate the image of Ken Tompkins with blood streaming from his nose. How could Betty have allowed this to happen? And with a married man! But then he hears Ken's voice, all unctuous charm and bogus concern. He planned it from the start, didn't he? Just as he planned that kiss on the beach. People used to refer to Ken as the black sheep of the Tompkins family but marriage to Olive has – so the story goes – reformed him. He rubs his fingers over his aching temples. From the few things Betty has let drop he's formed the impression she plans to keep the baby. More fool her, if that's the case. But if she's going to have even the smallest chance of making a life for herself and a child she'll need money, lots of it. 'You're right,' he says, stooping to touch his wife's shoulder. 'I'll see Lance tomorrow.'

Chapter Seven

'Our acts our angels are, or good or ill,
Our fatal shadows that walk by us still.'
JOHN FLETCHER

This is the life, my father tells himself, as the gates of the New Zealand Embassy on Observatory Circle swing open. Fancy free, anonymous, and money to burn. Not to mention the dream run he's having at the institute. After barely three weeks studying the data he is more than ever convinced that adding fluoride to the water supply will drastically reduce the number of dental cavities in children. School dental clinics are all very well, but filling the mouths of youngsters with black amalgam stands, in his opinion, on a par with putting a finger in the dyke to prevent flooding. Already he's made a start on his report, which will present not just the findings of his own research but the extensive data gathered over several years by his colleagues at the institute. Publication in the next quarterly journal should put the seal on his position as the country's leading expert in preventive dentistry.

'Ah, Mr Tompkins, telegram for you.'

My father smiles. He'd bet a guinea the telegram is in reply to the one he sent a couple of days ago to the New Zealand Dental Council. Mindful of the often bitter controversy surrounding the issue of fluoridation he had thought it only reasonable to inform the council of his findings so far. Not that he's ever been in doubt himself. Even without the conclusive evidence waiting to go into his report, he's known from the publication of the very earliest studies that fluoridation was the answer to New Zealand's abysmal record in dental health. Those stuffed shirts who persist in seeing the problem as connected to the mineral content of New Zealand soils will just have to find themselves something else to complain about.

He orders a whisky and sits down in one of several leather armchairs grouped about the room. As a visiting research scholar he has free use of the embassy's amenities. A generous supply of newspapers and magazines from home and abroad ensures he is never bored, and seldom homesick. He wired Olive on his arrival, since when he's written three airmail letters to her and is halfway through a fourth. He can't pretend she isn't on his mind – Jimmy Land's words *will* keep surfacing – but with so much hanging on the results of his time here he has no choice but to put anxiety aside and concentrate on his work. Some days he even forgets there's a war on! It's discussed, of course, in and out of the newspapers, but as far as he can tell its impact on the daily life of Washingtonians is so slight as to be negligible. The consensus seems to be that it's a European quarrel – regrettable, sure, but nothing to do with America. As for the women, maybe it's only true of this city, but the ones he's encountered so far strike him as being a great deal more worldly than their New Zealand counterparts.

'When the cat's away the mouse will play,' he'd teased, smiling at the charming woman who'd joined him for a drink last night at the bar favoured by his colleagues from the institute. With almost no one left to drink with, he'd been about to call it a day.

'You see yourself as a mouse?' the woman had challenged.

'I was thinking of you.'

'Were you now?'

Her name was – is – Barbara. Babs. Home town a little place no one has ever heard of in Illinois. 'Just like New Plymouth,' he'd joked. Babs was in Washington to attend a conference. When she leaned towards him he could smell her perfume.

'If I'm a mouse, then you must be a rat,' she'd teased back. 'A rat with sexy blue eyes.'

When he got back to his apartment he could smell her perfume on his fingers.

He decides to open the telegram over his second whisky. The thought of the number of people – some known to him personally – who will be incensed by his report puts a smile on his face. But as the words form in front of his eyes, his smile vanishes. 'IMMEDIATE RETURN IMPERATIVE STOP ACTION REQUIRED RE CHILD DUE IN MARCH STOP LANCE.'

His eyes swivel around the room. The only other occupants are a young couple studying the noticeboard. No one has seen his impulsive crushing of the telegram.

How dare you? he thinks, addressing the question to Lance. What business is it of yours? Then a worse thought strikes him. The only way Lance could have found out was if Betty, or that prig of a brother of hers, told him … Jesus … oh Jesus … Does that mean Olive knows too?

My father leaps up from his chair, knocking over his whisky. He doesn't see the startled looks on the faces of the young couple, nor does he reply when the uniformed man at the desk asks him if something is the matter. He doesn't see the wide sweep of Observatory Circle, or the brilliance of the lights illuminating the vice-presidential residence. All he sees is the cab, drawn up as if waiting for him. Once inside, he leans back and closes his eyes. It was all a terrible mistake, he's explaining to the wife he loves. I know I should have stopped it, but you can't imagine what she was like. I can barely credit it myself now. The kindest thing I can say about her is that she threw herself at me …

Chapter Eight

'But the present, like a note in music,
is nothing but as it appertains to what is past and what is to come.'
WALTER SAVAGE LANDOR

'You can rant and rave all you like, Ken, it doesn't change the situation. I'll spare you the moral outrage. You know as well as I do that what you did brings shame on us all. Never mind the initial folly of it, what in God's name made you think you could slip the net like that? Three months in Washington wasn't going to solve anything.'

'Yes, well I'm here now, so why don't you concentrate on the road and spare me the pieties.'

'Had a good time in America, did you? Plenty of nightlife?'

'What would you know about a good time? Perfect son, perfect husband, perfect father. Have you ever kicked over the traces, Lance? No, don't answer that.'

'We're talking about you.'

My father sighs. Less than an hour into their journey and still over a hundred miles to go. Initially grateful to his brother for coming to Auckland to meet him, he's beginning to wish himself anywhere but where he is, trapped in a car with no sign of his interrogation coming to an end. 'I sent her a hundred pounds,' he mutters. 'Credit me with that at least.'

'Not enough.'

'I don't agree.'

The car slows, then stops to allow a flock of sheep to cross the road. The chorus of bleating almost makes my father smile. Imagine this on Observatory Circle!

'I didn't force her,' he says, not looking at his brother, keeping his eyes firmly on the woolly creatures swarming around the car. 'If at any time she'd asked me to stop …'

'You're going to have to tell Olive,' Lance says.

'She doesn't know?'

'I didn't hear it from her if that's what you're asking.'

My father closes his eyes. Relief spreads through him like warmth after brandy. 'So it was Donald,' he says, but so quietly his brother doesn't hear.

*****

My mother stands in front of the long mirror in the passageway, gently massaging her bulging stomach, the voice of fear in her head temporarily silenced by the wonder of the new life growing inside her. She hasn't been to a doctor since that first traumatic visit in Wellington. But she doesn't need a doctor to tell her all is well. The baby dances inside her as if impatient to be born. 'Soon my darling, soon,' she murmurs, lulled by the silence in the house, and the half light of early morning, into believing the impossible possible, and her dream of a life with her child just a few weeks away from becoming a reality.

*****

Two weeks later my mother, wearing a curtain ring on her wedding finger, takes the train to Wellington. She sees no one in that city but hurries through the leafy evening streets to the wharf, where she boards the inter-island ferry. Arriving early next morning in the port of Lyttelton, she catches the first train south, alighting in the town of Timaru, overlooking the wide sweep of Caroline Bay. All she has with her are the sets of baby clothes she has made herself, the money my father has given her, and a suitcase containing her clothes. She is quite alone. Only Donald and his wife, and my father, know her final destination.

The date is 10 March 1940.

Chapter Nine

The day my mother leaves New Plymouth my father goes to work as usual, painfully aware, as he greets his first patient of the day, that this day is going to be anything but *usual*. He has given Betty five hundred pounds, a princely sum in those dark, wartime days. He has also paid for her confinement in a private nursing home in the South Island. Everything Lance required of him has been done, bar one thing – telling Olive. For nearly two months he has resisted Lance's repeated calls to confess. He's pleaded Olive's illness – diagnosed in early February as stomach cancer – insisting that the shock, despite the successful removal of the tumour, could kill her. He's berated Lance for sticking his nose in. He's insisted, more to convince himself than his older brother, that Olive need never find out, so why shatter her world? Isn't it bad enough that she may have only a limited time to live? For his part, Lance has accused him of wilful naivety. 'If you think your secret can be kept in a town this size then you're a fool,' he snapped during their most recent argument. 'I'm desperately sorry for what's happened to Olive, but she has to be told, and by you, not by some meddling friend. Wouldn't surprise me if she knows already.'

It's those words, plus the knowledge that Betty has left town, that have forced my father to finally acknowledge that his brother is right. Olive must be told. His eldest child will soon be starting school. Imagine if she were to hear some childish piece of gossip in the playground. Such things have happened before. He will do the deed tonight. He'll beg his wife's forgiveness, and assure her, with complete sincerity, that he loves her. And he will promise never to stray again.

The day drags interminably. Explaining to a patient – an attractive part-Maori woman in her twenties – the importance of daily flossing, he is overcome by a feeling of ennui so paralysing he stops, mid-sentence, and gazes out the window. Never before has he felt such a desire to sleep. The silent parade outside his window mesmerises him. What are these people hurrying to, or from? Where is that car going? What can possibly be so urgent to require such speed?

'Is something wrong, Mr Tompkins?'

He turns his body, to which invisible weights have been attached, in a half circle, and conjures up a smile for his patient. 'Thought I heard a siren,' he answers. 'Now, where were we?'

By the end of the day, dread has him by the throat. 'Be careful, young man. Your luck won't last forever.' The words – his father's – keep playing in his head; a stuck record that he would smash if he could. But his father was right. Youngest child of a close and loving family, handsome son of a doting mother, clever student whose exploits his peers could only envy, he has finally met his nemesis. Olive will have every right to send him packing. And won't his enemies just love that! 'PROMINENT DENTIST ACCUSED OF ADULTERY.' 'You were always jealous of me, Lance,' he mutters as he locks the surgery door behind him. 'Well, now you've got your revenge.'

*****

'Say something, Olive. For the love of God … Olive?'

My father bends over the prone body of his wife. It's the middle of the night. He almost wishes the baby would wake so he could leave the bed, and the sight of his wife's accusing back. But the baby has been sleeping through the night for weeks now.

'*Please*, Olive,' he begs again. (Why oh why did I do it this way? he is asking himself. All I've done is compound the cruelty.)

They'd sat together all evening, outwardly at peace, listening to the wireless, avoiding, at his request, the nightly news bulletin. What he had to confess was bad enough without the addition of the news from Finland – now in the hands of Germany's ally, Russia – or the latest outrage from Lord Haw Haw. Olive made no objection to the change in their nightly routine. Her only stipulation, when he said he wanted to talk to her, was that it not be about her health. Since her surgery the word *cancer* has been outlawed, as if, by refusing to name the disease, they could render it impotent.

It should have been possible to say what had to be said, but every time he got close his heart went into such a spin he was forced to stop and think about nothing but the next breath. Olive, sitting in her usual chair on the other side of the hearth, carefully taking up the hem of Gilda's new school tunic, was such a perfect Madonna he found himself thinking of angels, and wondering, irrationally, if one would come to his aid now. He knew how lucky he was to have Olive as his wife. Even by his own reckoning she was too good for him. That she seemed to love him as much as he loved her was nothing less than a miracle. How could he ever hope to explain what he had long persuaded himself was an unfortunate, but understandable, 'fall from grace'? It wasn't as if Olive was in the habit of denying him, though there were times, it had to be said, when her sheer goodness acted as a brake on his natural instincts. He'd take her in his arms, and feel such overwhelming tenderness for her his ardour would fade, and all he could do was hold her. At such times he felt he not only loved her, he worshipped her.

None of which, of course, made his task any easier, but still, it should have been possible … Olive is the angel in my life, he kept telling himself. She will see into my mind and heart, know I never meant to harm anyone, and forgive me. There is a beast in men, he would tell her, one that not even the best of women – and you, darling Olive, are the very very best – can subdue entirely. You must blame that beast for my 'fall from grace'.

In the end he'd said none of it. They'd checked on the children and retired to bed, as they'd done every night since Olive came out of hospital. Lying in his wife's arms, listening to her ragged breathing, he'd felt those same invisible weights that had hindered him in the surgery press down on him again, as if his unspoken confession had taken physical form. He heard the clock in the hall strike eleven, then twelve … He tried to pray but the words never made it past his throat. There were no angels to help him now, and no God. The God of the church he attended with his family had no time for sinners like him. Yet wasn't God the Creator of All, and the Creator, therefore, of the beast that drove men to seek – what? – excitement? connection? conquest? What he'd done, with its awful consequences, was nothing to do with his love for Olive. Surely she would see that. Surely to God …

He woke Olive as it was striking two. Out it all poured, before she was even properly conscious: the confession of guilt; the grovelling apology; the declaration of love; the pleading; the promises. There was no order to his narrative, only words tumbling over each other in his eagerness to get them out.

At first Olive could not grasp what he was saying. 'Has something happened to Betty James?' she asked, blinking at him in the semi-darkness.

'Yes,' he answered miserably.

'Why are you telling me this now? It's the middle of the night.'

'I'm sorry. I'm sorry, darling. I couldn't sleep …'

Olive yawned, pulled herself up, and leaned on one elbow. 'You'd better tell it to me again,' she said.

This time he told the story as a simple sequence of events. The special pleading would have to wait. He'd been unfaithful, he told her. It only happened once. (No need to mention Washington.) He'd been led on – not that that was any excuse, he added hastily – but it *was* an explanation. As a result, Betty James was pregnant. He was sorry, dreadfully sorry. He would do anything to turn the clock back, stop it from happening, but since that wasn't possible he felt the only decent thing to do was to tell her. She was such an extraordinary woman, with a capacity, like no one else he knew, to understand and forgive human weakness, she would see how essentially innocent he was. Never at any stage had he intended harm.

He would have gone on – there was so much more he wanted to say – but Olive put out a hand to stop him. At first he thought she was silencing him because she'd forgiven him, but then he saw, from the look in her eyes, that he was mistaken. She was looking *through*, not *at* him. After an agonising few seconds ('Be careful, young man. Your luck won't last forever') she turned her back, pulled her knees up to her chin, and closed her eyes.

*****

He wakes to an empty bed. For a moment he is blinded by the light, racing across the room as if in pursuit of sluggards. He looks at his watch. 7.45. He should have been up an hour ago.

Telling himself to stay calm, not assume the worst, he pulls on his dressing gown and walks with measured steps down the passage to the kitchen. The children are already up, the baby perched in her highchair, Gilda and Tony sitting at the table, their faces smeared with Marmite, their eyes popping as they turn to look at their dishevelled father.

Olive is standing at the bench buttering toast. She turns to look at him. There is nothing in her expression to suggest this is anything but a day like any other. 'Good morning, dear,' she murmurs.

'Get down,' Tony says cheerfully.

'Have you finished your toast?'

'Yep.'

'*Yes*, not yep.'

'Yes, Mum.'

'What about you, Gilda?'

Gilda glances at her father. Does she see what's written in his eyes? Or is her sudden frown because he's wearing a dressing gown and not his usual business suit? 'I'm finished too,' she says.

'All right, off you go. Brush your teeth,' Olive calls after them.

My father sinks into the nearest chair. The baby is busy distributing porridge around the tray of her highchair. What kind of God decides that the consequence of passion will be a small, gurgling creature with a talent for porridge throwing, he asks himself? Either the whole thing is a sick joke, or …

He never gets to finish the thought. 'I've made up my mind,' Olive announces, joining him at the table, calmly pouring him a cup of tea. 'We must adopt the baby. It's the right thing to do. It's your child, so it should be with us, part of our family … Don't look like that, Ken, I've thought it all through. We must contact Betty immediately, before she gives the baby away to someone else.'

Chapter Ten

....

'Now, gods, stand up for bastards.'
William Shakespeare

The nurse taking down my mother's details has a large brown mole on her left cheek. A single hair, carrot coloured, like the hair on her head, grows out of it. Betty wonders why she has never done anything about it. Guessing her to be about forty-five she tries to imagine her as a young girl, with freckles, and large, surprised-looking green eyes. She must have been pretty then, apart from the mole.

'You don't really think that ring fools anyone, do you?' the nurse says as she writes MISS in large letters before the words HILTON and JAMES.

My mother tries to swallow but the sudden constriction in her throat makes it impossible. 'You'll be well treated there,' Donald had assured her. 'You don't have to take Ken's word for it. I've made my own enquiries.'

'It's so far away,' she'd protested, knowing of course that that was the point of it. The further away from New Plymouth the better.

What had she imagined? That she would be able to pass herself off as married? Husband overseas perhaps? Or tragically killed in an accident? Whatever comforting illusions she'd conjured up were dust and ashes now.

'Father's name?' the nurse enquires.

Just for a moment my mother is tempted to break her promise. Why shouldn't Ken be exposed too? The word *feminism* is no part of her vocabulary, but the last nine months have taught her to question the universal admiration, in this century of war, for all things masculine.

She shakes her head. The nurse smirks. 'Present address?' she continues.

The contractions had started during the night. She'd lain on her bed in the Seaview Guest House, timing the gaps between pains, talking all the time to the baby she would soon be holding in her arms. Not until the gong rang for breakfast did she alert anyone to her state. Mrs McNaughton, the kindly widow who managed the guest house, fussed around her, holding her hand until the ambulance arrived, even offering to accompany her to the nursing home. 'Don't you fret now, Mrs James,' she comforted. 'Having a baby is the most natural thing in the world.'

Now, as one indignity follows another, my mother wishes she'd accepted Mrs McNaughton's offer. Perhaps the sour-faced nurse, ushering her into the bathroom, ordering her to strip while she runs a bath, would treat her differently if an older woman were in attendance.

'Mind you wash thoroughly,' the nurse cautions. 'There's a button on the wall if you need help.'

Left alone, my mother sinks into the tepid water and closes her eyes. The contractions have slowed down. Is that a bad sign? She wishes now that she'd read more about the actual business of birth, instead of inventing stories to carry her and her child into the future. 'I know it's not what you want to hear,' Donald had said to her the night before she left, 'but both Laurel and I hope you will decide to put the baby up for adoption. Please think about it, Betty. Think about the life your child would have, not knowing its father, living a hand-to-mouth existence …'

'You sound like Ken.'

'I hope not. I've no wish to see or talk to that man ever again. But I have been talking to Lance. You owe him a lot, Betty. It's because of him you have enough money to even consider …'

'Who else knows? Who else have you talked to?'

'Just the family. And Jean, of course. But you talked to her yourself.'

Jean. My mother clasps her hands over her swollen belly. It was Jean who wrote to her about Olive's baby, Jean who told her Olive was ill. Was it a mistake to contact her? The long hot weeks at her brother's house had almost sapped her will to live. She'd been determined to stay indoors, to see no one but Donald and Laurel and the children, but the day came when she had to get out. Besides, as Laurel had pointed out, it hadn't been possible to keep the truth from the children. Isobel, at nearly ten, was beginning to put two and two together. And Kelvin was asking questions …

No, Jean was not a mistake. Her visits to her house, the long talks they'd had, the drives they'd gone on together, had made her incarceration bearable. There'd been no question of walks in the public gardens, or along the sea-front, but there were places they could go where the chances of anyone recognising them were remote. 'But how will you manage?' Jean had said when Betty confided her plan to keep the baby. 'You said the father wasn't going to go on supporting you, so you'll have to work, won't you?'

I'll go back to Mrs McNaughton's, Betty answers Jean now. I'll get a job, find a place to live. I can type, take shorthand. With more and more men signing up to fight there will be plenty of jobs for women ... If it's a boy I'll call him Donald. If it's a girl I'll call her Frances ...

'Out you get, Miss James,' the nurse instructs from the doorway. 'Time to get you shaved.'

*****

Over the next twenty-four hours, as the contractions come and go, my mother is visited by a doctor, a social worker and a minister of the Presbyterian Church. All, with varying degrees of kindness, say the same thing. 'The best thing you can do for your child, Miss James, is give it up for adoption.' Pictures of the life her child would have with a respectable married couple, chosen for their irreproachable character and comfortable, even affluent, circumstances, are paraded in front of my mother's exhausted eyes. He, or she, will have a first-rate education, with opportunities to develop whatever talents he, or she, is born with. Surely Miss James understands there is no greater gift you can give a child than a respectable home. Stories of adopted children who have flourished in such an environment are legion. As are stories of children blighted by the taint of single parenthood. 'You should think very carefully,' the Reverend Newlands warns, 'before exposing your child to the cruelty of the world.'

As the contractions speed up, and the pain increases, these voices vie for dominance in my mother's head. She sees her son standing alone in a miserable back yard with no friends to play with. She sees him at school, taunted by his classmates. She sees him, bloodied and bruised, fighting off his persecutors. Then an even more horrible picture pushes those images away, and it's a daughter she sees, weeping with shame, turning her angry face on her mother, accusing her of ruining her life. 'You're no better than a … a …' She bats the word away, only to find that another, equally shameful, has taken its place. These were the words not said but implied by the doctor, the minister and the social worker.

*****

Early on the morning of 18 March my mother's long labour comes to an end.

'Oh, but she's beautiful … Look, Nurse, look! Isn't she beautiful?'

'I can only let you hold her for a moment, Miss James.'

'Do babies usually have so much hair?'

'It'll fall out. She'll be bald in a week.'

'Hello, Frances. Hello, my darling. Hello …'

'You need to give her to me now.'

'No!'

'For the baby's sake, Miss James. And for your own. Till you make your decision …'

'*Please* …'

The nurse prises my mother's fingers apart and lifts me out of her arms. This is not the nurse with the mole on her face, but a younger woman with kind eyes. 'Come along, Frances,' she says as she walks out of the room. 'No need to cry now. We'll take good care of you.'

Chapter Eleven

'There is no happiness in hatred.'
ALBERT CAMUS

The house belonging to Lance Tompkins, the uncle I never met, still stands on the banks of the Waikato River, and is, from what I could see of it on a recent walk along the river path, a large but unpretentious home, in which four children were raised by a loving father and a stern but affectionate mother. How I came to discover my father's identity is a story to be told later. It's enough, for now, to know that when I was forty-nine, five half-siblings came into my life. Three of them – Olive's children – I would grow close to; the other two, children of my father's second marriage, would, for different reasons, remain strangers. As for the roll-call of cousins, it's the four children of my Uncle Lance I have come to know best, and regard as friends.

At the time of my birth, Lance Tompkins was a QC. He would later become a greatly respected judge. I doubt he was ever told about his sister-in-law's wish to adopt me. Somehow I can't imagine the father I eventually met assenting to something that would not only publicise his 'fall from grace' but also, since I would be there as a daily reminder, ensure that it was never forgotten. My guess is that my father made up a story to explain to Olive why I could not be adopted into my biological family. Perhaps he told her my mother refused her offer (which I feel certain she would have done). Which makes it all the more puzzling that he chose to tell me, five decades later, that his wife had wanted to adopt me. Clearly it still rankled with him that she had had to be told at all. She was a sick woman. The cancer that had plagued her since before the birth of her youngest child would return, ending her life before Rayna, her baby, started school. She should have been protected from the truth, not had her nose rubbed in it. If it had been left to him she would never have been told of my existence. But my mother's 'interfering brother' had other ideas, as did his own brother. The fact that Olive would almost certainly have found out – New Plymouth, indeed New Zealand at the time, having many of the qualities of a village – seemed, when we spoke, to have been conveniently forgotten.

'There is no happiness in hatred,' Camus tell us. So I have to accept that my father, in his life-long hatred of my mother and her *interfering* brother, destroyed what chance he might have had of being happy. The little I know of his second marriage would seem to bear that out. But on that bleak autumn day, as his words slid into my ear, like the poison administered by Claudius, it was not sympathy I felt, but disgust. I couldn't wait to get away.

That meeting in 1989 in my father's house – not the house I have imagined, but a later one, where he lived with his second wife – was the only time we came face to face. My de facto stepmother, who had nursed Olive, then married my widowed father, made her feelings abundantly clear. I was never to visit again. She needn't have worried. Nothing would have induced me to repeat the experience. The irony of the situation only struck me later, when the waves of nausea that gripped me for days afterwards had lessened, and I could replay my father's words with something approaching calm. All this time it had been my mother I had been looking for, not my father. When I learned, two years before that meeting in New Plymouth, that my mother had died, I abandoned my search. But unbeknown to me a close friend (about whom, more later), went on looking. While I was still grieving the loss of the mother I had imagined so vividly, this friend, whose detective skills rival Miss Marple's, uncovered my father's identity.

As I stood on the doorstep of my father's house, struggling with words that seemed to have lost all meaning, my father squeezed my arm and whispered, so his wife wouldn't hear, 'If ever you need anything …' When I told my half-sister, Gilda, about this, she let out a small gasp of astonishment. 'Dad never talks like that,' she said. 'Gestures of affection from him are as rare as hen's teeth.'

So perhaps he was not all ice. Perhaps he was even deserving of sympathy.

Three years later he was dead.

Unable to love the father I had found, I took refuge in the thought of his brother, Lance, to whom it seems I owe a great deal. All the evidence points to him as the facilitator of my adoption. One of my cousins, Uncle Lance's second son, who followed his father into law and, like him, became a High Court judge, remembers overhearing a discussion about my father being 'up to his old tricks'. This time around, with serious consequences. The one thing not in dispute is that my adoption was arranged privately (a practice I described in my fiction long before I knew of its relevance to me), so I assume there was a correspondence between my uncle and the man who would become my legal father. In my fiction I imagined both men as Rotarians, hence the connection between them. It turns out they were both Masons. Whatever the facts, one thing is certain – nine months after my birth, I stopped being Frances Hilton James and became Elspeth Sandilands Somerville.

PART TWO: THE BEGINNING

'Nothing ceases to be, just because it has gone into the past.
Time is something we impose on the world.'
DMITRY LIKHACHEV

Chapter Twelve

'In the end all we can do is go back to the beginning.'
HOWARD BARKER, *VICTORY*

June 1940

The man standing on the balcony of Lauriston, the house that would be my home for the first eleven years of my life, is Thomas Somerville, a man more than entitled to put 'Esquire' after his name. He has come out to smoke his pipe, not through any concern for the non-smokers in the house, but because he likes to look out at the bay, and the city that has been his home for all of his sixty-eight years. The tide is in, so he is spared the sight of dead octopuses and drowned kittens in sacks. With water lapping in the inlet he can turn his gaze instead to the church spires, repeating themselves, like so many musical markings, across the city skyline. If his eyesight were better he might even be able to make out, behind the proliferation of buildings along the waterfront, one of the three factories he regards, with quiet pride, as his own. As a true son of a pioneering Presbyterian family he sees, in the smoke curling from chimneys, domestic and commercial, a sign that the world, despite the distant war, is in good hands.

On this particular morning Tom has a lot on his mind. Firstly, there are the practical matters to do with the war. He has been in business long enough to know he is bound to lose many of his best employees to the armed forces. Conscription, sooner or later, is inevitable. He feels no resentment about this. Inclined to the pacifist cause in the last war, he has no doubt that this war, against the evil of fascism, has to be fought. He may have hesitated over Spain, but not any longer. As an ardent supporter of the movement to promote World Federation he has had to acknowledge that what began in Spain is not going to end there.

The first thing to be done is to reassure those men who do sign up that their jobs will still be there for them when they return. The second is to start recruiting women. Tom smiles, takes his pipe out of his mouth and bangs it on the veranda rail. A trail of tobacco floats down onto the gravel path. While he busies himself refilling the bowl, he practises what he's going to say to his wife on this subject. When he married Alice, almost ten years ago, she was the deputy matron of a small private hospital. It was 1931, the beginning of what is now referred to as the Depression. His business – publishing (mostly books on local history), printing labels, making wax paper – like so many others was badly affected. Orders dropped off, profits plummeted. But not a single man was laid off. He took pride in that. As he did in the fact that his wife was not, like so many others, obliged to go back to work. She offered to. She even seemed to want to. But he insisted they could manage. The house was large, the garden even larger, but they would carry on as if nothing had changed. Alice would still have Joan (not her real name) to help her in the house, and he would have Robbie to keep the garden in trim. Neither of those good people would go without while there was still cash to pay wages.

So what will Alice say to his plan to hire women to work in his factories? It already has the blessing of his directors, but that will carry little weight with his wife. A woman of seemingly endless energy, he wouldn't put it past her to suggest she save him a salary by doing at least one of the jobs herself. Out of the question, of course, with a child (make that two, if things go to plan) to take care of. John, whose second birthday has just been celebrated, came into their lives in August 1938. The decision to adopt was mutual, but the driving force behind it was his wife's. He himself, with so many nieces and nephews, not to mention grand nieces and nephews, felt no great need to introduce a stranger's child into the mix. Not that he feels that way now, but with Lauriston for so many years the scene of regular Sunday lunches, sometimes with as many as twenty, half of them children, sitting around the table, he would have said, if asked, that his life was complete as it was. Truly 'my cup runneth over' were the words that often came to him on these joyous Sunday occasions. The Lord had shepherded him through his years of darkness; now here he was with a wife who knew, better than anyone, what his journey had been, and how hard won these days filled with light.

That Alice should want a child of her own was only natural, living as she did among a mêlée of Somerville relations. That he'd hesitated, even if only for a moment, was something he regretted now. Not a day went past when he didn't remind himself how much he owed her. What other woman would have accepted what she had silently assented to from the first day of their marriage?

The eldest daughter of a large family, Alice had taken her role as mistress of Lauriston in her stride, but that hadn't stopped him worrying. None of her own family lived nearby. Surely she must be lonely? But as the months, then years, went by he came to understand, with relief, that the Alleys were not nearly as interdependent as his own clan.

Without wanting to be uncharitable, Tom hopes the Alleys will continue to keep their distance. His father-in-law (the phrase makes him uncomfortable; there's only a few years between them), a man he has yet to see with a smile on his face, fathered eighteen children by two different wives. The very thought of all that bedroom activity makes Tom feel queasy. These days, much to the relief of his many children and grandchildren, Henry Alley has more or less withdrawn from the world, content to forget the names of his offspring, while remembering the names of every horse he ever had dealings with. His fame as a horse trainer – or 'horse-whisperer', as some call him – means little to Tom. Some of the horses he trained went on to win important races, a piece of information Tom chooses not to dwell on. Horse racing, along with all forms of gambling, is, in his view, up there with the Seven Deadly Sins.

Whenever he thinks of his father-in-law, which admittedly isn't often, Tom is troubled by the fact that the man describes himself as a Christian. Being Irish, it would not have been surprising if the Alleys had been Catholic, but they're not, they're Protestants, like himself. Only they are not *like* at all. The Alley version of Protestantism seems to have nothing to do with belief in a loving God. Perhaps that explains the somewhat chequered mental history of some members of the family. Several are, if not certifiably mad, then close enough to sound alarm bells, and of the sane ones, at least two call themselves communists. One of his wife's cousins has taken himself off to China, where he is fast making a name for himself as a teacher and general trouble-maker. Another has earned a more acceptable notoriety as an All Black. A half-brother is a Baptist missionary, serving in the Solomon Islands. Two more, survivors of his father-in-law's first, doomed marriage, can best be described, in the wake of their experiences in the Great War, as 'walking wounded'.

Not wishing to dwell any more on his in-laws, Tom draws deeply on his pipe and sets off to find Robbie. Whenever he has something on his mind it's Robbie he turns to. As often as not they end up talking about nothing more pressing than the relative merits of King Edward potatoes over Desirees, but the end result is always the same – he feels calmer, clearer in his mind. He knows where he'll find Robbie – in the vegetable garden. 'Robbie's domain', as it is affectionately referred to. If he were asked to describe his relationship with his gardener he wouldn't use the words employer/employee, he would use the word *friend*; he might even, with a grin, use the word *marriage*. Over the years he and Robbie have arrived at a perfect division of labour: Robbie looks after the vegetables and the lawns; he takes care of the flower beds. Not much given to introspection, Tom admits to himself that if he were asked to define happiness, his garden, his pipe and Robbie would all loom large in his answer.

'Again and again and again/ Again and again and again, again/ My wife she died and I laughed and I cried/ For I was single again.' He's been singing this song for as long as he can remember. 'Better not sing it in front of your wife,' his sister Bessie snapped in the wake of his announcement that he was going to marry Alice Alley. To this day he doesn't know why his decision caused so much distress. Alice may have been an Alley but she was a highly respected nurse, who had carved out a life for herself in spite of her domineering father. Not that that cut any ice with Bessie, who'd kept house at Lauriston during his long bachelorhood. He would have thought she'd be glad to relinquish her role and have an establishment of her own to run. But all these years later she still refers to her departure from Lauriston as a 'banishment'.

He rounds the end of the veranda and sets off along the path. The sound of the gravel crunching under his feet is reassuring. With so much changing in the world it's a comfort to see, hear and smell things that have been part of his life since infancy. The bank to his left has been mowed for winter. The smell of freshly cut grass, more imagined than real, tickles his nostrils. Tucked into the hollow at the bottom of the bank is the greenhouse, one of the many additions he's made to the property. He grows tomatoes there, but it's the rows of lovingly tended begonias that give him the greatest pleasure. There's something voluptuous about their large orange and pink and yellow petals: as if God decided to make a flower that would rival the splendours of a Victorian lady's hat!

The glasshouse is the place Tom retreats to whenever an atmosphere he can neither decipher nor explain builds up in the house. He'd hoped these 'storm warnings', as he's taken to calling them, would lessen, even disappear, with John's arrival, but the opposite has been true. Not that there has been any change in the treatment *he* receives. Alice is meticulous in her care of him. But that hasn't stopped him feeling, at times, as if he is the interloper, not the boy. He loves the child, of course. His sisters are always telling him what a 'softie' he is where children are concerned. But he can't shake the feeling that there isn't room for him in this new domestic dispensation. Mother and son speak a language that is foreign to him. They make noises at each other; exchange secret smiles; seem mysteriously joined even when physically separate (how else to explain Alice's uncanny ability to know, even when at a distance from the child, that he is upset?). It's a puzzle, that's what it is. He wonders if any of it is his fault.

Rather to his surprise Alice showed no interest in adopting a daughter. He would have thought, having lived so long among women when she was a nurse, she would have been happier raising a female child. But she held out for a boy, resisting him – was it really for the first time? – when he expressed his own preference for a girl. It's that resistance that's troubling him now, as he makes his way through the gap in the hedge to the rose garden.

He can hear John's gleeful shouts from inside the house. Riding his tricycle up and down the corridor, no doubt. He should be playing outside. A bit of cold wind never did anyone any harm. But Alice likes to keep him near. That he and Alice were allowed to adopt at all was something of a miracle. Most couples, given his age (Alice is twenty years younger), and the shadow of mental illness hanging over her family, would have been rejected at the first hurdle. He's still not sure why this didn't happen. He doesn't like to think that the decision came down – as his sisters keep telling him – to his 'standing in the community'.

Pausing to snip a dead rose head, Tom feels a brief pang at the thought that it may soon be his patriotic duty to dig up these flower beds and plant vegetables, a sacrifice made once before, during the Depression. He won't mind too much losing the dahlias or the marigolds or even the hydrangeas, but the rhododendrons on the slope leading down to the orchard took years to establish, as did some of the more exotic shrubs nestling in the shade of the greenhouse. Perhaps he will be able to keep the Cecil Brunners, trained to cover the avenue of arches he and Robbie built two summers ago. And no one surely will expect him to dig up the climbing roses that scatter white petals, like summer snowfall, over the dark macrocarpa hedges.

Tom straightens his back and tosses the dead rose into the garden. 'Most people marry in order to have children,' Alice had pointed out the first time the subject of adoption came up. He'd nodded, unable to think of anything to say. The idea that what was unspoken between them might have to be spelled out had rendered him speechless.

With a quick shake of his head Tom dismisses the memory and continues along the path that leads to the vegetable garden. He can't see Robbie through the opening in the hedge but he's prepared to bet he'll find him there, digging up potatoes or weeding around the leeks. With luck they'll have a large enough crop of spuds this year to feed not just his own extended family but Robbie's as well. He'll take Robbie's advice about what to plant in the spring, bearing in mind that the production of food will soon be taking priority over everything else.

Turning his head to the right he can just see the tip of the slope behind the henhouse. Come springtime it will be covered with daffodils. Will he have to dig those up too? Behind the bank, out of sight from where he's standing, are the two garages that house his faithful old Tin Lizzie, bought when he was a bachelor, and the Plymouth he uses these days to drive to and from the city. He's toyed with the idea of retiring now he's approaching seventy, but with the war showing no sign of coming to the promised swift end, not to mention a child to support, those plans have had to go on hold.

Sure enough, Robbie is in the potato patch, talking to himself as he wields his spade. What he's saying will be known only to God. No one has ever been able to decipher Robbie's murmurings.

'Smoke-oh!' Tom calls.

Robbie waves his spade in the air. 'Rightyouare,' he calls back.

They'll talk first about the things they both understand – the best time to plant runner beans, the right amount of lime to get the best out of the camellias. Then he'll raise the subject that has been on his mind to the exclusion of just about everything else for the last three days. 'What would you say to a little girl running around the place? A sister for John. Sound like a good idea to you?'

Robbie won't answer for a while. He'll know his opinion is not really what's being asked for. He'll chew on his cigarette, and nod a few times. He might even take off his hat and run his hand through his tangled, salt-and-pepper hair. Then he'll say something like, 'Nothing beats a daughter. Even now I can see my Mavis running about in her singlet, giggling like a banshee. Best years of my life, when she were little ...'

Yes, Robbie will know what to say.

Chapter Thirteen

'It's late for living, late for loving
For fathoming the sky,
Understanding the world.'
PRIMO LEVI

'What?' Alice says, dropping the sock she was darning into her lap. 'I don't understand. I thought we agreed. One child is enough.'

Tom runs a finger over his moustache, a habit of his when needing time to consider his response. He and Alice are sitting by the fire in Lauriston's sitting room. The wireless is on, playing the music Alice likes to listen to. Mozart, she said it was when he asked. Music is his wife's department, not his.

'We're not getting any younger, Tom.'

'I'm not, that's for sure,' Tom laughs.

'We've been lucky with John. We may not be so lucky a second time.'

Tom turns his head so that what he is seeing is not his wife's frowning face but the room he has known since childhood. How often has he sat in that window seat, doing the daily crossword? How often has he joined in family sing-songs around the piano? Alice has never expressed any wish to change anything in this room, or indeed anywhere else in the house. Those are Somerville photos on the sideboard, Somerville pictures on the wall ... Given the poverty of her background, and the sheer hard labour of her life as a nurse, he'd always assumed she was grateful for the relative comforts of Lauriston. But what if she wasn't? What if that frown signalled not just her reluctance to adopt another child but a deeper malaise? 'I don't think luck comes into it in this case,' he says gently, turning back to his wife, smiling at her. 'We know this wee lassie. We know her family.'

'You know them, Tom. I don't.'

'Lance Tompkins is a fine chap. He'll be a judge one day, mark my words.'

'But he's not the father, is he?'

Tom clears his throat. Not much given to irony, he acknowledges its presence in the current situation. The last time he and Alice discussed adoption, she was the one doing the pleading. The trouble is, he doesn't have the words. In the past, when he took risks he wouldn't dream of taking now, he could be fluent in the language of emotion, but these days he marches to a sterner drum. Admitting he feels as if he already loves the baby Lance described in his letter would bring scorn down on his head, even if it does happen to be the truth. So how is he to persuade Alice to agree to what Lance is proposing? It's a big step, no doubt about that, but he'd hoped to impress her with his description of what a fine family the baby – healthy, according to Lance, and graced with a sunny disposition – hailed from. That was a mistake. Alice may have taken his name but she was still an Alley. Her sympathies were with the underprivileged, not with a family of lawyers and dentists anxious to distance themselves from scandal. He'd have been better off telling her the baby had been found abandoned on the orphanage doorstep.

He takes off his glasses and rubs his eyes. Alice has resumed her darning. He watches as the needle goes in and out, weaving the threads together to make a perfect pattern. He's long since stopped urging his wife to relax, to take up the kind of hobbies – crosswords, card playing, reading, sun-bathing – that give his own life flavour. Alice doesn't know how to relax. Not even on holiday. The nearest she gets is when she sits down to read to John.

'The child is called Frances,' Lance wrote. 'It's the name her mother gave her. She's being cared for in the Truby King Hospital just up the road from you. I have a passing acquaintance with the child's mother, whom I remember as a young girl. She's a good woman, Tom, from a good family. So far she has refused to sign over the baby for adoption, but I feel sure that would change if she knew you and your wife were interested … I'm only bringing this up because of something you said last time we met – that you wished the baby you and your wife had adopted had been a girl …'

'I know what you're thinking,' Tom says, repositioning his glasses and smiling at his wife. 'We thought it about John, didn't we? We both know how these children come into the world. But once you held John in your arms those thoughts vanished. It will be the same with this wee lass. She will become your daughter.'

The look Alice gives him causes him a momentary pang. Has he said the wrong thing again? Is it possible his practical, no-nonsense wife regards their son as miraculously conceived? Not a second son of God – not even Alice, surely, would go that far – but born without stain. 'All I'm trying to say –,' he begins, but Alice cuts him off.

'How children come into the world is of no interest to me,' she declares.

Tom nods. 'Nor me,' he agrees. 'They are all God's children.'

'You've set your heart on this, haven't you?'

Tom waits a moment before replying. If he says the wrong thing again it could ruin everything. Alice's kindness to him, miraculous as it often seems given the sternness of her nature, is not something he has ever taken for granted. Besides, he doesn't want her to agree to the adoption to please him. He wants her to want it as much as he does. 'A sister for John,' he urges. 'That would be a good thing, don't you agree? We were both brought up in large families …'

He pauses, wondering if this is the right moment to mention her early life, spent, if what he has been told is correct, looking after her many young siblings. She herself never talks about that time. What information he does have has been gleaned from his infrequent contact with her numerous siblings, and from things his own family, far from happy about his choice of wife, have imparted to him. But one thing he does remember. 'She was tough on us girls,' her youngest sister, Vera, told him. 'She expected us to work as hard as she did. Which meant from dawn to dusk! The boys had their chores, but by comparison they got off lightly. And if they did something wrong she'd make excuses for them …' Should he be worried about that? Did her reluctance to adopt have more to do with the sex of the baby than the fact of it being a second child to take care of?

'I know you, my dear,' he says softly. 'You're far too modest to take any credit for the raising of your many brothers and sisters, but I've had it from the horse's mouth that you were more of a mother to them than your stepmother ever was. And I've seen with my own eyes how marvellous you are with John. Can you blame me for thinking you are the mother this poor wee lass needs?'

Alice leans her head on the back of the chair and closes her eyes. The music has come to an end. The announcer informs them they have been listening to the Jupiter Symphony. Next will come the news, none of it good.

'Switch it off, shall I?' Tom suggests.

Alice opens her eyes. She looks at the sock on her lap, then at him, then back at the sock. 'You say her name is Frances,' she says.

Tom nods. Frances Hilton James, he thinks, but doesn't say, in case that too offends.

'I don't like it. Makes her sound like a boy.'

Tom clears his throat. 'We can change it,' he says. 'Just as we did with John. What would you like to call her? Perhaps you'd like to name her after one of your sisters.'

'I don't care what she's called, so long as it's not Frances.'

*****

Closing the door behind her, Alice stops for a moment, listening for signs that her son is awake and needs her. But all, in this isolated house, is silent. The wind that has been bothering the windows for the last three days has stilled. The only sounds are the ones she is making herself as she pads her way across the hall, down first one corridor then another, to the kitchen. Nine o'clock. Time for Tom's final cup of tea of the day.

She fills the kettle with water, places it on the range, throws another shovelful of coal on the glowing embers, buttons up her cardigan against the chill of the rest of the house, and walks out of the room again. There is only one person who can calm the erratic beating of her heart, and that is her son.

The sight of John's black curls on the pillow brings a smile to her face. She has never tried to explain to herself why she loves this little boy so much. There's never been any need. From the moment she first saw him in his crib she knew she wanted him. It has nothing to do with the years she spent looking after her father's second family. Tom was wrong about that. Being obliged to take care of so many sad little infants didn't turn her into a mother; it made her resolve never to have children at all. The day her father told her she had to leave school in order to help her stepmother in the house was one of the darkest days of her life. School was her refuge from the constant demands of the woman she blamed not only for her mother's death but for her father's frequent rages. Now she would be at her beck and call twenty-four hours a day. By the time she was in her twenties the family had moved five times, always to an even more remote piece of land, which her father, venting the fury inside him, would attack as if Nature itself were his sworn enemy. And still the babies kept coming.

She reaches over the cot and gently pushes back the damp curl clinging to John's cheek. One of her half-brothers is called John but that's not why she chose the name. She loved her siblings, but not as much as she loved Fred, Harry, Clarice – children of the same sweet mother as herself – and not, by a long chalk, as much as she loves her son. She would never want to escape from John, as she had wanted for so many wasted years to escape from the children clinging to her skirts, their eyes huge with fear when Father was in one of his moods. How could she explain to Tom that John was all she wanted, all she had ever wanted? She had no desire for a daughter. She didn't know why that was. If she bothered to think about it at all she simply assumed it had something to do with the woman she had been told to call 'Mother', but managed mostly to call nothing at all. A woman of stern appearance and manner, who addressed her husband as 'Mr Alley' and spoke in platitudes: 'A place for everything and everything in its place'; 'The Devil finds work for idle hands'. Of course she knew her stepmother wasn't really responsible for her mother's death, but she'd lost no time taking her place, which was almost as bad.

The day she finally escaped that life (she was twenty-eight) she could hear her stepmother in the kitchen upbraiding one of the children. 'Waste not want not. How many times have I told you, money doesn't grow on trees.' That particular altercation, hardly unusual in itself, was not what drove her to pack a bag, wait for dark, tiptoe out the door and walk five miles to the nearest neighbour, but it was what came back to her when her efforts to blank out the past failed and the memory of that day came flooding in.

'You don't want a sister, do you, my darling?' she whispers, stroking her son's hair. On impulse she reaches for the scissors, kept out of harm's way on top of the wardrobe, and snips a curl from the top of his head. She knows where she's going to put it – next to the photo of her mother kept in a locket that no one, not even Tom, has seen. 'A silly little girl running around the place. We don't want that, do we?' She carefully tucks in the covers – the nights in this draughty house are freezing –

and places a feathery kiss on her son's cheek. 'But your father has set his heart on it, and I'm afraid that means …'

She doesn't finish the sentence. Back in the kitchen she pours boiling water onto the tea leaves, swirls the pot three times (Tom insists he can tell when she neglects to do this), arranges the cups, and a plate of Tom's favourite sultana biscuits, on the trolley, and heads back to the sitting room. With that family's blood in her veins she's bound to be a proper little madam, she thinks as she pushes the door open with her foot. Well, I won't stand for any nonsense. I'll treat her as I treated my probationer nurses. That'll knock the silliness out of her.

Chapter Fourteen

'Time present and time past
Are both perhaps present in time future,
And time future contained in time past.'
T.S. Eliot

The Truby King Harris Hospital, like the orphanage that was its near neighbour, no longer exists. These days it's known as the Every Street Lodge, providing budget accommodation for travellers. No doubt some of those travellers are drawn to the address: just a few doors down from the hospital stands the vacant site of the infamous Bain murders. But in 1940, when I was taken, by whoever in those days handled such things, to live in the hospital, it was an imposing two-storey building forming a wide semi-circle on the brow of a hill. The sign at the gates announced that visiting hours were Wednesdays and Saturdays from 2.30 to 4. I like to imagine that my mother, unwilling to give me up for adoption, chose to visit at those times, but I have found no evidence to justify that belief.

The regime laid down by Dr Truby King, founder of this and other children's hospitals throughout the country, was strict. A health reformer, with experience in the treatment of mental patients (he was for a time superintendent of the 'Seacliff Lunatic Asylum') Dr King had early on in his career become a believer in the theory of eugenics, which at the time of my birth was being used by the Nazis to justify some of the worst crimes in human history. But only the more benign aspects of the theory were evident in the treatment prescribed for babies and children in Dr King's 'Karitane' hospitals, so named in honour of the small Otago settlement where he and his family lived. 'SAVE THE BABIES' was the slogan on the outside of the building; 'kind but firm' the rule of thumb inside. Babies were to be fed regularly but on no account were they to be fed 'on demand'. Bowel movements were expected to be regular. Daily bathing was mandatory. Overt displays of affection were discouraged. Doctors and nurses were admonished to stick to the timetable and follow the routine. Only through order and discipline would children learn the essential lessons of self-control and self-denial.

These were the rules that governed my life from my birth till my adoption in December 1940.

So who were we, the children filling the wards of the Truby King Harris Hospital in Andersons Bay, Dunedin? Were we all sick, or was there another reason for the rows of cots, where infants exhibiting no physical reason for distress were, by order of the superintendent, left to cry? Discovering my own connection with the hospital in my forties, when I was engaged in the search for my mother, changed forever my view of the place. Prior to that discovery I'd simply thought of it as somewhere babies were sent to when they were sick.

The fact that I know anything at all about those first months of my life is thanks to a woman I used to see every Sunday, sitting in the same pew beside her father in the Andersons Bay Presbyterian Church. Her name was Margaret Dunlop and she was, to my childhood eyes, a regal figure, straight-backed, perfectly groomed. Given to making up stories to counter the tedium of the long, declamatory sermons, I invented a narrative in which Margaret had been engaged to a handsome soldier who was killed in the trenches of the First World War. As an expert eavesdropper I had heard several such tales. All I had to do was add pledges of eternal devotion, leading either to a rapturous reunion at the end of the war, or its beatific counterpart in heaven, the fate I ascribed to Miss Dunlop.

Margaret knew all along what my origins were. She may not have known the identity of my birth parents, but she was a nurse at the Karitane hospital, and knew I was not a sick child but an illegitimate one. One of the things I would discover, when I began looking for my mother, was that until the late 1950s illegitimate births were recorded separately from legitimate ones. But if that was intended to distinguish bastards from those born without stain, I doubt it had any impact on Margaret. I believed her when she said she took a special interest in me, though I don't imagine she went so far as to disobey the rules. 'Overt displays of affection' would have got her into trouble.

I met up with Margaret in 1986, the year I returned to New Zealand to look for my mother. I'd not seen her since childhood. As we talked in her elegant sitting room, it was if the language of the 40s and 50s had become an invisible barrier, one we had to break down in order to get at the truth. 'I can't tell you whether your mother visited you in the hospital or not,' she told me, in answer to my question. That it pained her to say those words was evident in the spots of colour that had appeared on her perfectly powdered cheeks. 'She may well have tried to see you when I wasn't on duty. But I can tell you such visits were frowned on, even prohibited in one case I remember. They were considered disruptive, bad for the child.'

But I didn't come away empty-handed. As I was leaving, Margaret handed me an envelope containing a montage of baby photos of myself. 'I broke the rules the day your parents took you away,' she said. 'I shed tears.'

It wasn't the first time I'd been confronted with the evidence that other people knew, or thought they knew, more about my origins than I did. At various times I'd been told I was the daughter of an officer in the Indian army; that I had a Jewish mother; that I was the heir to a great fortune. Tempting though these scenarios were, they paled alongside the fantasies I had been inventing for myself ever since I was old enough to put words and ideas together. Looking back, I believe it was these fantasies that prevented me for so long from searching for the real people in my story. How could real people hope to compete?

I cannot now remember how I came to be aware of Margaret's role in my early life. The search for my mother involved many false starts and blind alleys. But I do remember going to the Dunedin headquarters of the Plunket Society (another of Truby King's creations) to look up my records. I had by that time established that I had been an 'inmate' in the Karitane hospital in Andersons Bay, records of which were stored with the Plunket Society. On being told that the records for 1940 had been destroyed in a fire, I admit to thinking, for a few distracting weeks, that some kind of conspiracy to hide the truth of my identity was the only possible explanation. I'd already allowed my imagination free range in my fiction (*River Lines*, which I wrote before knowing the facts of my birth, was to prove eerily prescient), but here was the evidence that someone somewhere had something to hide. That illusion was only shattered when I met my father, not an impoverished poet, or a war hero, or a clergyman with feet of clay – the candidates of my fantasies – but a dentist.

Thinking myself back into the mindset of that time, with a war no one wanted to fight about to engulf the whole globe, I can see how natural it was for people to keep secrets. The government had no need to exhort its citizens to keep their mouths shut ('LOOSE TALK COSTS LIVES'): discretion came naturally to a people known for their modesty and reticence. As for the citizens of Dunedin, no one could live up to the high standards set by their Presbyterian forebears, but they could, and did, keep quiet about the all too human lapses that occurred. That way the values most people still believed in could be maintained. Little wonder my search for information about my origins felt like the proverbial search for the needle in the haystack.

But I did have one precious window on the past – the photos gifted to me by Margaret: three faded black and white images pasted onto cardboard. Written at the top is my name, 'Nan' (short for Frances), and the date (the wrong date, as it happens). The largest photo is of Margaret, in her starched white uniform, holding me in her arms. The caption underneath reads, 'The day "Nan" went Home'. Below that is a group photo, with Margaret holding me again, taken on the steps of the hospital. Smallest of the three is a photo of me lying stark naked on a mat, kicking my legs in the air, grinning as if my life depended on it. Was that where I learned that if I were to survive I had to please? Margaret is no longer here to ask, but I suspect the answer to that question is yes.

*****

I had one further contact with the Truby King Hospital, one I don't remember except for the moment that brought that contact to its spectacular end. Piecing together what happened from things my Somerville relatives have told me, I assume my parents, Tom and Alice, had gone away on holiday, taking John but leaving me, aged three, in the care of the nurses back at the hospital. Where my parents had gone, and for how long, I've not been able to discover. The day my father came to collect me I was being brought to the reception area by a nurse. The only explanation for what followed is that I must have spotted my father through the glass door that separated the wards from the hospital entrance. I let go of the nurse's hand and hurled myself through that closed door and into his arms. I have no memory of cuts, or blood, or the sound of breaking glass, just the sensation of utter joy as I catapulted into the arms of the man I adored.

Chapter Fifteen

'... the point is to live everything.
Live the questions now.'
RAINER MARIE RILKE

When, in my mid-forties, I began seriously to look for my mother I insisted, to anyone who asked, that my reasons were to do with health – I was tired of being asked by doctors if hives, which my daughter suffered from, ran in the family, or if there was a history of heart disease. (I had recently been plugged into an ECG machine at the John Radcliffe Hospital in Oxford, where I was living at the time. The cause of my 'ectopic heartbeat'? Too many mugs of strong black coffee!) But of course I knew that a far deeper malaise, one I was not willing to acknowledge at the time, lay behind my decision. My marriage to Bruce Purchase had come to an end. The fallout was painful, especially for my teenage son. As one more or less sleepless night followed another I found myself thinking more and more about my mother, till I woke one morning knowing I couldn't delay a moment longer. I had to go back to New Zealand and look for her.

Timing, they say, is everything. My daughter was in her last year at Warwick University. The conviction that she had a bright future ahead of her, despite the upheavals I had subjected her to, was not just a comfort to me, it enabled me to contemplate time away from England. My troubled son had recently become a weekly boarder at Lord Williams' School in Thame. For the first time in almost two years he was happy and settled. A visit to his head of house reassured me that not only would he be accepted as a full-time boarder for the second part of the current term, he would be well looked after. Had I known then what I learned subsequently – that his father had failed to pay the fees as stipulated in our separation agreement – I might not have left England with such ease of mind. But the school in its wisdom decided to leave me in ignorance.

*****

By the end of February I am back in my home town, Dunedin, staying with my cousin Jack, a Presbyterian minister, and his wife Janet. They know I am here to search for my mother and are warmly supportive. Janet, a solicitor, offers to appear for me in my application to the court to be allowed to see my original birth certificate. I accept gratefully. While we wait for the date of the hearing to come around I stick my nose into as many pies as I can, chasing the records of the Plunket Society and the Karitane hospital (I can't remember who told me I was once a Truby King baby: it feels like something I've always known), quizzing anyone I consider likely to have relevant information, visiting Margaret Dunlop.

The day of the hearing is fine and sunny. The harbour, viewed through Jack's large picture window, sends off sparks. I can see Andersons Bay where I grew up, and the adjacent hills where I hiked with friends. The soldiers' memorial, splintered years ago into my memory, is a poignant silhouette on the ridge known as Highcliff. I feel as if those hills, with their peaks and troughs, their shadows that dip and dive into the sea, live inside me. If I stare long enough, I tell myself (not for the first time), I will de-code their mystery, and understand why they awaken in me such a deep sense of longing.

Janet is optimistic. In six months' time the adoption laws will change, and adoptees will be able to access their birth information without recourse to the courts. The legislation to make this happen is already in place. But I will not be here in six months' time. My marriage may have ended but my life in England has not. So we go to court, confident that the judge (his name is Twaddle – 'straight out of Dickens,' I whisper to Janet) will let me see what I will soon be entitled to see, with or without his permission.

But Judge Twaddle has other ideas. He listens to Janet's submissions, reads the documents we have filed in support, asks me a couple of questions, then rules that as I am clearly of sound mind (am I supposed to be grateful for that?), with a clear sense of identity, he sees no reason why my birth certificate should be made available to me.

It's all over in a matter of minutes. Janet and I walk out of the courtroom, Janet muttering rebelliously, I silent beside her. When we reach the reception area Janet grabs my arm and says, 'Wait here.'

'What?'

'I'll only be a few minutes.'

I watch her scurry back into the courtroom and disappear through a side door. I'm too upset by what has just happened to think about anything else. Whatever she's gone to do, it won't change the verdict.

True to her word she's back within minutes. In her hand is a piece of paper which she passes to me. 'If you ever tell anyone about this I'll be de-barred,' she says, glancing over her shoulder to be sure she's not being overheard. 'You can't do anything with it, but at least you have what you came for – your birth certificate.'

I glance at the paper but the words won't stay in place. All I see is a series of grey smudges surrounded by white edges. 'Is it …?'

'The original? No. I'm not a thief. Fortunately I know my way around this place. It's a photocopy.'

I look at her in astonishment. This is a side of my cousin I have never seen before.

'I figured the judge would head for his room,' she says, pulling on my arm to hurry me out the door, 'leaving the documents for the clerk to file. I was right. All I did was borrow one page from his bundle.'

I look again at the page in my hand. 'Frances Hilton James …' I read. 'Born Timaru … Mother Betty Hilton James, born Stratford, Taranaki … Father Unknown.'

I try to say thank you but a trapdoor seems to have sprung shut in my throat.

Janet smiles. 'You do understand what I'm saying, don't you, Nookie? (she calls me by my family nickname). You can't do anything with it.'

I nod.

'Good. Then I think we deserve a drink.'

Next day I travel to Wellington from where I will leave, the day after, for England. I'm to stay with Jennie, my best friend from primary school, and her husband Martin, a television reporter. Of course I tell them about the hearing, and the shock of Judge Twaddle's decision. I don't tell them what Janet did, only that she acted for me, but when, under pressure from Jennie, who was as sure as I was that the hearing would go in my favour, I admit that I actually have my birth certificate, the rest of the story slips out. Panicking, I swear them both to secrecy. Only when they've both promised half a dozen times to say nothing do I calm down.

Jennie asks to see the document. Now that I'm satisfied Janet's reputation is safe again, I'm more than happy to share the information that has been spinning around in my head for the last twenty-four hours. Frances was the name I had wanted to write under. At the time my first novel was published the women's movement was in full swing in Britain. Virago Press had been set up by the excellent Carmen Callil. It was a great time to be an author who was both young and female. But something stubborn in me (my mother would call it 'cussed') kicked against the idea of being seen as part of a movement, even one as admirable as feminism. I wanted to be judged simply as a writer, without reference to the current wave of excitement about women's liberation. Frances, I decided, would give me just the right hint of androgyny. My publisher disagreed. 'You'd have to spell it with an *i*,' he pointed out, 'and that would be false representation. From where I'm sitting you're definitely not a man.'

I lost that battle, but there was a part of me that continued to think of myself, every time I sat down to write, as Frances.

Jennie is still staring at the document. There's an odd expression on her face, as if something's not quite right. 'What is it?' I ask her.

'Your mother,' she says. 'She was born in the same year and the same town as my mother. Stratford's not big. Hardly even a town. What's the betting they knew each other? I'm going to ring Mummy and ask her.'

'No!' I say, snatching the document from her. 'You can't do that. You can't do anything. I promised Janet.'

'But it won't be you doing it,' Jennie says.

'And *you* promised *me*.'

'What harm can a phone call do? I won't mention your name. Nor Janet's. I'll just say I met someone who mentioned Betty James, and I wondered if Mummy knew her. What's wrong with that?'

We go on arguing, but my heart isn't in it. The possibility that someone might be able to tell me something about my mother is too great a temptation.

As I listen to Jennie's voice on the telephone I begin to understand the meaning of the expression, 'her heart leapt into her mouth'. After she has explained why she's ringing, a silence opens up. I try to read the look on her face but it's no good. What can I possibly infer from that small, concentrated frown, and the occasional nod or half-breathed word? I glance at Marty, who flicks me a conspiratorial smile. What I am seeing, although I don't know it yet, is the birth of a joint detective operation that will combine Marty's skills as a researcher, learned in the corridors of Television New Zealand, with Jennie's expertise at asking loaded questions while looking as if butter wouldn't melt. With quiet persistence she will question not just her mother but others connected to the town and the date on my birth certificate. She will not rest till she finds answers.

'Betty James,' Jennie's mother is saying into that silence. 'Whatever happened to her? She was my best friend at school.'

Chapter Sixteen

'All happy families resemble one another but
each unhappy family is unhappy in its own way.'
LEO TOLSTOY

'**Say hello to** your sister,' my father instructs his two-year-old son. 'Her name's Elspeth.'

'Ethpeth,' my brother murmurs.

'Clever boy,' my mother encourages. 'Such a difficult name.'

'Elspeth is how we say Elizabeth in Scotland,' my father declares proudly. 'What do you think of that?'

'You can call her whatever you want,' my mother whispers in John's ear.

They are standing around the cot that had been John's and is now mine. My mother has done everything expected of her. She's sterilised the bottles used by John; brought the pram out of storage; taken the linen, blankets, piles of nappies and baby clothes out of the chest and hung them on the line to get rid of the smell of mothballs. No new clothes have been bought. That would be extravagant. As for the baby gowns embroidered by Betty, they have long since been passed on to other Truby King babies. Nothing that connects me to the woman who gave birth to me has survived.

'So what do you think?' my father asks my brother. 'Do you think she's pretty?'

I imagine John staring down at the gurgling creature with flyaway hair and busy blue eyes, and thinking she looks like a rather large, rather ugly baby bird. 'Ethpeth,' he says again.

'Right, that's enough,' my mother decides. 'We follow Dr King's regime in this household. Six o'clock, near enough. Lights out.' She takes John by the hand and marches him out the door.

But my father lingers behind, unable to tear himself away from the sight of the wee miracle who is now his daughter. He's lost count of the months since the arrival of Lance's letter, with its improbable proposition. Securing Alice's agreement was only the start. After that had come a seemingly endless exchange of letters and phone calls till the necessary papers were signed, and the next stage of the adoption process – a hearing to establish whether he and Alice were fit to be parents to Baby Frances – could begin. The adoption may have been arranged privately, without reference to government agencies, but due process still had to be observed. Tom knew it would help that he and Alice already had a child, but that didn't stop him worrying. The first time he saw the baby – the only one he had eyes for – lying in her cot in the Karitane hospital, he felt such a surge of love that the thought of her going to any family but his almost brought him to his knees. He'd always thought of himself as a lucky man (what had gone wrong in his life in the past had been his own doing, nothing to do with Luck or Fate), but on the day the baby became his he felt as if God Himself was smiling down on him. A new birth certificate was issued, and Frances Hilton James was given the names he had already, with Alice's indifferent agreement, chosen for her – Elspeth Sandilands Somerville.

As I imagine that day, my first in Lauriston, I sense both my father's happiness and the shadow, in the form of his anxiety about his wife, that will in the end overwhelm both him and me. He knows Alice only agreed to this adoption to please him. Everything about her behaviour up to this day confirms his suspicion that she is acting out of duty, not love. The contrast with the day they brought John home could not be starker. But he refuses to be downcast. Alice is a good woman. He only has to think of all she has done for him to be reminded of that. Her refusal to be enchanted doesn't mean she won't grow to love the child. Give her time, he thinks, smiling down at me.

'God bless you, Nookie,' my father says, laying his warm hand on my cheek, bestowing on me the nickname he was given as a child. 'Sleep tight.'

*****

But what of my other mother, my *real* mother as I cannot help but call her? What did she feel as she signed away her baby (the only one she would ever have) for adoption? How did she react to the cold finality of that life-changing document?

I don't know what Betty did or where she went after she gave birth to me in Timaru. All I know is she paid for my keep while I was in the Karitane hospital. But something, stronger than mere wishing it to be true, tells me she did visit me in the hospital. Nor was that the end, because she visited me at Lauriston. I have some evidence for this, though I doubt it's the kind that would stand up in court. That evidence – a battered silver bracelet made for a child – is sitting in front of me now.

What I remember is this. There were many visitors to Lauriston as I was growing up: uncles and aunts and cousins; business colleagues of my father's; fellow Presbyterians; strangers brought home by my quixotic father, who couldn't bear to think of anyone eating alone. But one visitor stands out – a woman who always came on her own and never stayed long. I can't describe this woman but I can *feel* her. She took a particular interest in me, but that isn't why I remember her. It was the chill with which my mother spoke to her on her last ever visit that has stayed with me, words I may have imagined, but hear as if they were spoken only yesterday. 'I must ask you not to call again. It's too upsetting for the child.'

The woman bends down to kiss me. There are tears in her eyes. She puts the tiny silver bracelet on my wrist and tells me she will always love me. I never see her again.

*****

In *The Stone Gods*, Jeanette Winterson, another adoptee, spoke of the search for the mother as a search that never ends. 'You never stop looking. That's what I found … I live an echo of another life.' When I learned, in a phone call from Jennie, taken on the set of the Agatha Christie film I was working on in England, that the woman who had given birth to me was no longer alive, something in me died too. My search had always been about my mother. Loving my adoptive father as I did, I'd never even been curious about my birth father. So when I recovered from the shock I told Jennie that was it: the search was over. Fortunately she ignored me. Had she not done so this story would be even more of a fiction than it already is.

Thanks to Jennie I know that my mother married in 1946, and that the marriage, from all reports, was happy. Her husband, Ken Gray (another Ken!), was a farmer from Southland. Armed with the information Jennie provided I was able, on my return to live permanently in New Zealand, to find the house Betty and Ken lived in in Invercargill after their retirement from farming: a wooden villa painted in vivid reds and yellows, with a wide veranda on three sides, surrounded by a large colourful garden. Was the garden my mother's creation? Were the bright colours her choice? There was no one to answer these questions, but I like to think some of the things Jennie had discovered about her – that she was an active member of the Invercargill Repertory Society, loved parties, was a good dancer – found expression in that rainbow house.

My mother never had another child. A close friend of hers whom I met in Melbourne (another small miracle facilitated by Jennie) told me everyone assumed Betty was barren. 'That's how it was in those days,' she said. 'No one thought to blame the man.'

'Yet here I am,' I answered her.

'Yes, here you are.'

Had I had my wits about me on that hot Melbourne day I would have asked my mother's friend if she thought Betty had told her husband about me. The fact that I didn't strikes me now as cowardice. I didn't want to hear what I suspect might be the truth: that my mother, in her new life as a respectable married woman, kept me a secret from everyone, even the person closest to her. If – as I have so often imagined – I had turned up on the doorstep of her Invercargill house, instead of the joyous reunion I had dreamed of, a very different scene might have played out, one not dissimilar to the painful meeting with my father. Just by existing I could have spelt the end of that happy marriage …

Then again, maybe not. Something another friend of my mother's told me (this meeting facilitated by one of my foster mothers, the wonderful Margot Ross) leads me to think that the preferred ending to this story may not be mere wishful thinking. What this friend revealed was that my mother was an active member of the Plunket Society, the organisation founded by Truby King to take his gospel to the wider world. Her devotion to the cause of infant health – she was described as a 'tireless worker' – suggests that she never stopped thinking about the child who spent the first nine months of her life in a Truby King hospital. I'll never know, but I can allow myself the hope that in working to save the lives of other babies, my mother was remembering, and grieving for, her own.

My mother and her husband died within six months of each other. In the year before their deaths they had suffered a painful loss. Four years earlier they had agreed to take care of two little girls, daughters of Ken's recently widowed brother. My mother's Melbourne friend described to me the happiness those girls brought to Betty's life. 'They were the children she never had.' So when, four years later, the children's father married again and moved to Wellington, taking the girls with him, my mother must have been desolate. Six months later she was dead.

Did she die of a broken heart? Did Ken? I can ask the questions but I can't answer them. I've not been able to discover the cause of my mother's death. She was sixty-two years old.

*****

I see my mother (my birth mother) standing in her garden, her face framed by scarlet rhododendrons, her back turned to the house so that her husband won't see the tears in her eyes. It's Sunday, the day Brian (I've invented the name) comes to take the girls out. But Brian isn't coming today.

Ken has suggested going on a drive. It's what they usually do to pass the time while the girls are with their father. But doing what they usually do will only serve to remind Betty how *unusual* this day is. It's not that she doesn't enjoy doing things with her husband. For nearly two decades, before the girls came into their lives, doing things with Ken was what she enjoyed most. 'Oh, you two lovebirds,' their friends used to tease when they were caught holding hands, or blowing kisses to each other. But all that changed when Rita and Ngaire (more invention) became, in all but name, their daughters. Not that they stopped being 'lovebirds' – they would always be that to one another – but their love changed, became something they wore with greater solemnity than before. It was as if what had been missing in their lives had suddenly, miraculously, been supplied, and the question they never asked one another – why have we not been blessed with children? – could be swept away with the autumn leaves.

But this is not an autumn day but a spring one. And Brian won't be bringing his daughters back at tea time because he's taking them to Wellington to live with him and his new wife.

'Four years, Ken. That counts for something, doesn't it? And Brian away for much of that time.'

'Don't, darling, you'll only make it worse.'

'Ngaire calls me Mummy. She always has.'

'Well, she was only six when she came to us.'

'Even Rita ...'

'Stop it! Please, Betty. Brian is their father. He has rights which we've never had. We always knew this day might come.'

'*I* didn't.'

'We have to put on a brave front. For the girls' sake.'

'Why? They're not here to see us.'

'We'll be writing to them and they won't want to read that we're sad. And we can speak to them every Sunday. Brian has promised us that.'

'They didn't want to go. You saw the way Ngaire clung to me.'

'All the more reason for us to stay cheerful.'

Betty looks back at the house, where the man she has loved for a quarter of a century stands anxiously watching her from the veranda, and a terrible thought enters her head. It's your fault we never had children. You are the barren one, not me. But she'll never put that thought into words because it would mean telling him so much else, and that, she long ago resolved, must never happen. The only people who know her secret are her family, in faraway New Plymouth, and the man responsible for the best and worst thing that ever happened to her. For despite the shame, and the lonely years that followed, she can never be sorry that Frances was born.

'Be in in a minute, dear,' she calls out.

Ken lifts his hand to his lips and blows a kiss. 'I'll put the kettle on,' he calls back.

She can hear the relief in his voice. He too has been dreading this day, not just for its anguished farewells, but for what it might do to her. But she won't let him down. She will be stoic. She knows how to do that. She's been in this place of loss before.

There are so many things she wants to say to her husband, all of them involving the word love. I know you will miss the girls too, I know you loved them every bit as much as I did. But what you don't understand, dear, can never understand, is that my pain is deeper, older than yours. It goes back to a day in 1940 when I held a newborn baby in my arms, and allowed myself, for a few precious moments, to believe that love would be enough.

If only … If only I'd told you, right at the start, when you took me to dinner in that ridiculously grand restaurant in Wellington. A blind date, organised by Violet. I so nearly didn't go! I sensed straight away you were someone I could love. I should have said the words then, while there was still time. I've had a child, a daughter. The sentences shape themselves in her mind as they have so often over the years. I wanted to keep her, tried, but there was nowhere I could go … no one to turn to … The father was, is, of no importance. I didn't love him and he didn't love me. It was all a dreadful mistake except for … except for Frances …

Frances … Elspeth, the name that was given to her. Where is she now? For the first few years of her life she was able to see her. Tom Somerville, the kindly man who adopted her, raised no objections to her visiting. In fact he encouraged it. 'No such thing as too much love,' he said to her. But he didn't make the rules in that household; his wife did. At the first opportunity, in the absence of her husband, Mrs Somerville brought the visits to an end. After that she had to rely on titbits: tiny items of gossip from people who knew the family, the occasional mention in the paper of Frances (Elspeth) as she made her way through school and then university. The last thing she knew for sure was that Frances had married – her photo was in the *Otago Daily Times*. The ceremony was held in the Andersons Bay Presbyterian Church where Mr Somerville (dead by this time) had worshipped all his life. There was a rumour the marriage hadn't lasted. She hoped it wasn't true. They'd looked so happy in that newspaper photo.

'A secret once told is no longer a secret.' But it was too late now. Besides, there was the promise she'd made to Mrs Somerville, to never again try to make contact … If she told her secret she would be one step closer to breaking her promise.

As she moves back across the lawn, Betty rehearses the words she will say to her husband. We will get over it, she'll say. The hurt will lessen. The girls were never ours to keep. And at least we know where they are, and who they are with, and that they are loved …

What she won't say is: The worst thing, the very worst, is when your first thought on waking every day is that the child you love lives in a house where the word 'mother' brings not comfort, but fear …

Life goes on. A cliché, but one that bears repeating. 'Come my love, it's a beautiful evening, let's walk in the garden. Smell the fragrantissima. And the jasmine. See where the primroses have come up under the silver birch. If we're quiet we might hear a bellbird. They're hard to see, but you can usually hear them this time of day. I saw waxeyes a few minutes ago, a pair of them, skittering through the blossom. And look, here comes a fantail, hoping we'll stir up insects for his tea. I do believe he's flirting with us … Try not to be too sad, dear. Life goes on. It just does.'

*****

It's November 1991. My cousin Jack and I are driving to Invercargill. I have the address of the house where my mother lived, and the record of her burial, alongside her husband, in the Invercargill Cemetery.

Jack, whose resemblance to my father is a guarantee of my love for him, is a past Moderator of the Presbyterian Church, well known for his liberal stance on public issues. He was a passionate spokesman for the 1960 'No Maori, No Tour' campaign, committed to ending sporting ties with racist South Africa, a stance he maintained, despite family division, when the Springboks came to New Zealand in 1981. His defence of Lloyd Geering, a fellow minister, in the latter's infamous heresy trial of 1967, put him at odds with many in the church, as did his subsequent opposition to the senate's decision to exclude homosexuals from the ministry.

I am immensely proud of Jack. A decorated war hero and member of the exclusive Order of New Zealand – that he should be willing to take the time to drive me to Invercargill to lay flowers on my mother's grave has touched me deeply. His backseat driving, when I take the wheel, is less to my liking (he has often referred to me as his 'flighty' cousin), but we manage to laugh about it when we finally stop for tea and sandwiches.

We visit the house first. Jack wants to knock on the door but I prefer to peer over the fence, and imagine the life my mother lived there. I don't want to be told those vibrant reds and yellows, and the eye-catching garden all dressed up for spring, are not hers.

As we drive away again I turn for a last glimpse of the only tangible evidence that my mother once lived in this southernmost city in New Zealand. I no longer believe in the after-death reunions I used to imagine for my war-separated lovers, but I have a sense, strong enough to bring comfort, of something surviving of her love for me, and mine for her.

Twenty minutes later we are standing by my mother's grave. A small metal plaque tucked in among others lining the border of a well-tended garden marks the place where her ashes are buried. 'BETTY HILTON GRAY BELOVED WIFE OF KENNETH GRAY' it reads. Next to it, no more than a finger's width away, is a plaque with the words 'KENNETH GRAY BELOVED HUSBAND OF BETTY'. That and the dates are the only memorial to my mother and the husband she loved.

I place my flowers between the two graves, and ask Jack to say a prayer, though at that point in my life I'm not sure who, if anyone, will be listening.

I don't remember what Jack said, I only remember the feeling of peace that came over me as we walked, with our arms around each other, away from that place of death and flowers.

PART THREE: PLACES

'Half to forget the wandering and the pain,
Half to remember days that have gone by,
And dream and dream that I am home again ...'
THOMAS ELROY FLECKER

Chapter Seventeen

'Everything one was to become must have been there, for better or worse.'
A Sort of Life

I would like to say that Lauriston, the house which more than any other contains 'what I was to become', stood on top of a mountain overlooking the Otago Harbour, but that would not be true. It's how it felt, not how it was. From the front balcony you could see the Andersons Bay inlet, and the long causeway with the bridge in the middle that separated inlet from harbour, but though the approach to the house was up a long winding drive, it was not a mountaintop you reached at the end of your journey but a plateau halfway up a hill.

Not that there was much in the way of flat land. Scrabbling up steep banks covered with rosehip and blackberry bushes, roly-polying down the grassy slope at the front of the house, dawdling to school over bumpy paddocks smelling of pine and horse shit, clambering into huts clawed out of the lower branches of macrocarpa hedges whose tips touched the clouds – this was the physical world I inhabited, day after wild day. What flat land there was was given over to the growing of vegetables – 'enough to feed half a dozen families,' my father liked to boast – and the flowers he delighted in: the Cecil Brunner roses; the bossy dahlias and show-off peonies; the scented stock and prim-faced marigolds; the bold pink and blue and white hydrangeas, whose colours he arranged as if he were Monet creating the perfect garden; the tiny primroses in the rock garden; the rhododendrons, where my brother and I hid from Nazi soldiers; the daffodils that appeared each spring, as if by magic, on the slope behind the henhouse. There had been a tennis court once, hiding discreetly behind a tall black hedge, but the Depression and then the war had put an end to such frivolity. Not even the hint of a white line survived the arrival of potatoes, carrots, parsnips, pumpkin, cabbage (so many cabbages!), brussel sprouts, leeks, broad beans, runner beans, lettuces ... 'So long as we live at Lauriston,' I can hear my father saying, 'no one in the family will go hungry.'

*****

Andersons Bay, the suburb over which Lauriston, by virtue of its elevated position, presided, took its name from the first European to build a house in the area – James Anderson. No one seems to have thought to commemorate the true 'early settlers', Ngai Tahu, who deeded the land to the Scottish invaders. Street and house names, in this outpost of Scotland, read like a roll-call of its Presbyterian pioneers and the places they hailed from – Glendinning, Glenfalloch, McAndrew, St Kilda, Somerville, Portobello, Anderson, Waverley, Musselburgh ... The occasional Maori name – Tainui, Kaikorai, Otakou, spoken with difficulty by the Bay's sturdy citizens, fell from the tongue like a mumbled protest.

When the tide was out the bay presented a gloomy aspect to anyone standing on Lauriston's balcony. Even the naked eye could detect, among the remaining eddies of water, the discarded tin cans and broken buckets, the hanks of rope and slurries of rotting vegetation, the pale, worm-like strings of dead octopuses, the sacks of drowned kittens, snagged on the rocks. When the tide was in, dinghies were cast off from the shore, and fishing lines trailed over the causeway bridge, but it was what lay beneath that stayed in the memory. Depending on the wind the stench rising from this watery necropolis would either reach the nostrils or be carried out to sea. But once smelled, never forgotten.

One of several recurring nightmares I had as a child featured this toxic inlet, and the causeway that separated it from the harbour. I'm standing on the balcony at Lauriston, looking out over the inlet, when suddenly a bus packed with passengers, but with no driver, lurches silently into view. (I have yet to experience sound in a dream: is this normal, I wonder?) The bus, which is bringing people from the remote peninsula settlements into the city, moves steadily towards the bridge at the centre of the causeway. I leap to my feet and begin signalling frantically to the passengers but they can't see me. Nor am I able to utter a sound. I wake, knowing that every person on that driverless bus has drowned, and it's my fault.

Many years later, while struggling to free myself and my children from an abusive marriage, I dream of the inlet again. I'm back on the balcony at Lauriston, looking down on the bay with the tide out, and its fetid cargo starkly revealed. Standing beside me is the man who has been our family GP in England. Robert Beazer is an exceptional doctor – a man who taught philosophy at Oxford before switching to medicine and going into general practice. I trust him implicitly. We're not speaking or looking at one another, just staring at this place of death and waste. Then Robert says, 'Jump!' I look at him in horror. 'Jump!' he says again. So I do. But as I sail through the air I see that what I am diving into is not a rancid graveyard, but clear blue water.

*****

'How do I know what I think until I see what I say?' E.M. Forster wrote. Is that why I'm feeling, as I write these words, an uncomfortable mix of excitement and unease? Lauriston was not my first home – that dubious honour belongs to Truby King's Karitane hospital – but it's the first I remember. Long before I was made aware of the facts of my birth, I had appropriated the stories associated with the house on the hill and made them my own. Recalling those stories now is the cause of my excitement. Knowing I have less right to them than those who were born into the family is the cause of the unease.

The family into which I was adopted was one of the oldest settler families in the province. The name Somerville was respected throughout Otago. My father, and various of my uncles and cousins, held prominent positions in the business world, as well as being pillars of the Presbyterian Church. Adoption was unheard of in the family. What need was there to invite cuckoos into the nest, when families of five children and more were the norm? During my childhood more than one 'concerned adult' saw fit to remind me of my cuckoo status. Though nothing was said – presumably because little was known at the time – about the pre-John Knox family ancestry, the fact was that the Somervilles could trace their line back to William the Conqueror. Sir Gualter de Somerville, a Norman knight, was rewarded for his part in the defeat of the English King Harold by a grant of land, and the Barony of Whichenour and Burtone. A century later, after a legendary feat of valour on the part of one Sir John Somerville (he was said to have slain the 'wode worme of Laristane' – the serpent of Lauriston), a further barony was added, in Scotland. And so the Scottish House of Somerville came into being, along with a coat of arms commemorating Sir John's heroic deed. A far cry from the railway employees and small-time farmers who left Scotland for New Zealand seven centuries later, but the shadow of that elevated past could still be seen in the proud bearing of those intrepid pioneers.

Fortunately I knew none of this during the eleven years I lived at Lauriston, otherwise I might have been tempted to identify with that 'wode worme' slain by my putative ancestor. My father was not a boastful man. His pride lay in his family's more recent exploits: the decision of his grandfather to support the Reverend Thomas Chalmers, whose break with the established church over the issue of state patronage led to the setting up of the Free Church of Scotland; the long voyage to the other side of the world, prompted above all by the desire for religious freedom; the founding of a dynasty, and a church, in Dunedin, the 'Edinburgh of the South'.

As I listened to my father's stories, they became my story. I was there on that momentous day in 1843 when Thomas Chalmers led the rebellion that would result in the founding of a new church. I was there when my dissenting grandparents, Janet and John (first cousins as it happened, but no harm seems to have come from that), and their nine children, stepped aboard the barque *Blundell* for the five-month voyage to an unknown land on the other side of the world. I was there when they disembarked, in rain and high winds, at Port Chalmers. I was there when they spent their first night on the ten-acre section they'd purchased before they left Scotland, sleeping under a rough shelter built of branches. I was there as they listened in wonder to the noisy chorus of bellbirds and tui, kaka and robins, wild pigeons and parakeets. I was there as, gasping in astonishment at the sights and sounds assaulting their senses, they tried not to stare at the tattooed Maori sailors helping to carry their luggage. I'm not sure how present I was at their daily Bible readings and prayer sessions, or on the arduous weekly trip by boat to First Church on the other side of the harbour. The watered-down version of these events which I experienced as a child – compulsory church and Sunday school attendance; embarrassing prayer sessions with terrifying Uncle Harry Renfree – rather got in the way of my imaginative recreation of family worship a hundred years earlier.

But I was there when they built their first home, Charlesfield, and later when my grandfather (of whom more anon) built Lauriston. Since Charlesfield was at the bottom of the hill and Lauriston at the top (or almost), the logic of geography dictated that the former was called 'Down By' and the latter 'Up By'. Both names were still in use when I was growing up, but as 'Down By' was the home of the dark-suited Uncle Harry, who'd married my father's sister, I thought of it not as a family home but as the residence of an alarmingly different breed of human being altogether.

*****

I owe a lot to my gentle grandfather, William Somerville. Not only did he build Lauriston, the house I dream about still, but he was the reason, once I'd moved to England to live, that I could get a British passport. When I presented his birth certificate to the official at the passport office in Petty France Street in London, there was a stunned silence as the hapless man digested the fact that the young woman standing in front of him had a grandfather born in 1832, the year of the Great Reform Act. Conscious of his disbelief, I explained that my father was sixty-eight when I was born (no need to say anything about adoption), which put his birth back deep into the 19th century. From there it was no great leap back to 1832. Is it any wonder I have spent so much of my imaginative life recreating the past?

William, who was by all accounts a modest man, somewhat under the thumb of his formidable wife, Marion, nevertheless possessed qualities essential to the pioneering life. He could turn his hand to almost any occupation: school teacher, farmer, hedger, ditcher, sawyer, bush-feller. His building of the house that was to become the symbol of family unity and mutual support stands to this day as a testament to his many skills (though sadly, despite strenuous efforts on the part of one family member to redress the situation, Lauriston is no longer in Somerville hands).

William and Marion had nine children, the fifth being my father, Thomas Sandilands Somerville. When it came to naming me I was given not just my father's surname, but his middle name as well.

Chapter Eighteen

'We look at the world once in childhood
The rest is memory.'
LOUISE GLÜCK

Something strange happens to houses once they've lodged in the memory. Like Alice, when she ate the cake and grew six feet, they expand. For over two decades I lived on the other side of the world. When I came back, and went to visit my childhood home, not only was it lived in by strangers, it had shrunk! The house I remembered was a vast Victorian mansion, with intersecting corridors, stained glass windows and dark, seldom-used rooms, with heavy velvet curtains and a smell I identified as the scent not just of things hidden away from the light but of secrets. What I saw, on that emotionally charged return visit, was a modest-looking single-storey house, no longer sitting in splendid isolation among its many gardens but crouched on top of an unremarkable hill, its view over inlet and harbour interrupted by the forest of houses that had sprung up in my absence. Where was my father's hunger-defying vegetable garden? Where the orchard, and the transformed tennis court? What had happened to the paddocks and the cloud-tipping marcrocarpa hedges? Where were the garages, sheds, glasshouses? The unpretentious slate-roofed house in front of me was a mirage, a copycat doll's house, not the real thing at all.

Yet I only have to close my eyes to bring back that other Lauriston, to see myself running through the gaps in the hedges that separated one garden from another – flower beds closest to the house, then vegetables, then compost heaps and seed beds. Or walking with my brother across the paddocks linking Lauriston with another Somerville house, Gladsmuir, home to my Uncle Jim and his family. At other times I might be skipping down the steep, rhododendron-lined path that led to the orchard, where the greatest secret of all – an overgrown air-raid shelter – lay hidden under the spreading branches of an apple tree. It was there my brother and I would spend long summer afternoons hiding from the Germans (the Japanese, who posed a far more immediate threat, were for some reason considered less interesting), checking our supplies of tinned food and water, dressing our imaginary wounds as we bravely repulsed the enemy and saved the nation. Walking back up through the trees, gorging on the fruit we were forbidden to pick, my brother would peel off to seek distraction in one of the disused garages, home to, among other treasures, an old Tin Lizzie, which he boasted he would restore to full running order as soon as he'd saved enough pocket money. I would go indoors, worried that so long an absence may have got me into trouble. If I was in luck, and my mother hadn't registered the time, I would creep out again, drawn by the mystery not of old cars and garages, but sheds housing tools, sacks of flour and sugar, an old saddle and bridle (fuel to my obsession, in the wake of reading *Black Beauty*, with horses) and, most precious of all, a doctor's leather bag, complete with coloured bottles, rusty instruments (tweezers, scissors) and a rubber, mask-like contraption whose purpose I hardly dared imagine.

These days architects talk about the inside/outside flow of a house, something that would have made no sense to the builders of Lauriston. Outside was another universe: a place in which to create an alternative reality. My brother and his 'gang' had a hut that I was not supposed to know about. My best friend Jennie and I had a hut that *he* was not supposed to know about. There were so many places to hide it was possible to be lost for a whole, dreaming afternoon. When it was time to come back for a meal my father would step out onto the balcony and blow on an antique Swiss horn, used in another century to summon cows to the milking shed. (I regret now that I never thought to ask him how he came by such a thing. Like the wine glasses from Florence, and the carved chest from Japan, and the mahogany furniture from England, there must have been a story attached to that Swiss horn, one that would have afforded me a precious glimpse into the sixty-eight years my father lived before I was born.) The horn made a strange melancholy sound, rather like the sirens that were let off every day across the water to mark the end of factory shifts. I knew better than to dawdle when I heard that peremptory summons. The need to stay on the right side of my mother was the spur that sent me flying across the paddocks.

The moment you entered the house everything changed. Shoes were removed in the large porch where coats and hats and scarves hung like the ghosts of past adventures. The porch was brown – brown walls, brown linoleum, large brown broom cupboard, where I once hid to escape my mother's wrath. Other rooms had different auras, different predominant colours that seemed, to my darting eye, to change as the fluctuating emotional moods of the house changed, but the porch stayed brown, a colour I have disliked all my life.

If I could draw, which I can't, I would have no trouble recreating every one of Lauriston's rooms. Nothing that went on there seems now to have been in the least ordinary. Everything is imbued with significance. I can't explain this except to say that this is what memory does – peels away the trivial to expose the deep seam of meaning underlying everything we do. According to Günter Grass, memory 'is like an onion that wishes to be peeled so we can read what is laid letter by letter'. So here I am, at the entrance to the house, ready to peel back the walls of its many rooms, and live again the life I had there.

*****

I see the kitchen first, entered from the porch. My mother is there, bent over the sink, her thin, apron-wrapped body tense with concentration, her lips clamped tight as she scrubs the wooden bench to within an inch of its life. The sleeves of her dress are protected by plastic sheaths which she has made herself. Dirt is her constant enemy. How can she ever hope to find peace when people keep walking on her scrubbed floors, and spiders insist on spinning their webs in high, unreachable corners?

On the table behind my mother is the jug of carrot juice she has prepared for my father. It's my job to wash and peel and grate the carrots (muddy from the garden, with bright green feathery tops), which she then strains through muslin to provide my father with his daily dose of vitamins. Perhaps it is also to help him see in the dark? My brother has told me carrots were grown during the war and fed to pilots to help them navigate at night. When I'm older he will enlighten me about radar, and British attempts to hide the fact of its existence from the Germans, but on the day I'm remembering I see that jug of carrot juice as nothing less than an immortal elixir. My father, thanks to my mother's daily ministrations, is going to live forever.

The kitchen is huge – it isn't of course, but this is how I remember it – with a coal range (my brother remembers it as electric, but I see a bucket full of coal and a long-handled shovel), bench and sink under the window, table and chairs at right angles to the bench, and a pantry, stacked with my mother's jams and preserves, tucked into the back wall. It was only when I had children myself that I began to realise, and be appalled by, my mother's workload, running a house built in the nineteenth century, with a kitchen that hadn't changed since the First World War, and a copper in the washhouse to boil sheets and towels. A nurse before her marriage, my mother acted as if Lauriston were a hospital that had to be scrubbed and ready for inspection at any moment. When years later I saw Genet's play *The Maids*, I recognised, in the character of the Madame donning white gloves to check the furniture for dust, my dirt-obsessed mother. At various times a woman, usually a relative, would live in to help with the housework, but with the bar set so high few lasted more than six months. Only Joan, whom I hold partly responsible for a lifetime of constipation (she told me if I pushed too hard on the lavatory I would have a baby) stayed long enough to seem like a permanent member of the family.

It's late morning, a Saturday, or perhaps a day in the school holidays. I've already attended to the carrots, so now my job is to peel the apples that have been brought in from the orchard. While my mother scrubs potatoes and cuts up cabbage, I struggle with the peeler that seems determined to take off smaller and smaller pieces of skin, till my mother, enraged by my lack of progress, snatches the instrument from my clumsy fingers and does the job herself. She doesn't smile. She seldom does unless it's at my brother, whom she loves more (I think even then) than my father. I'm afraid of my mother, mortally afraid, but it's her sadness that frightens me most. She is the saddest person I have ever seen.

The colour I associate with the kitchen is green. Walls, pantry, floor, the formica table, the chairs where we sit to eat our morning porridge (though not my father – he has breakfast in bed) are all a smudgy shade of green. Above my head is a clothes-horse. It squeaks and snaps every time the door opens. It has the strangest garments hanging from it: collarless shirts, dusty pink long-johns, woollen shorts, viyella pyjamas, lisle stockings, knitted spencers, shapeless flannel underpants and a wide elastic bandage.

Since it's clear my mother would rather I wasn't in the room I sneak out past the pantry and along a narrow corridor to the hall, the 'hub' of the house. Everywhere I look there are books – Dickens; Thackeray; Walter Scott (the complete works); Defoe; George Eliot (to whom I will discover many years later I am, by birth, distantly related); the gleaming gold-leaf edition of *The Seven Pillars of Wisdom*; books about John Knox and the Highland Clearances; tales of missionaries toiling in the sun; art books (one of which, to the shocked delight of my brother and me, contains pictures of nude women) – books I will read long before I can understand what I'm reading.

I see my brother and me playing marbles in the hall. A quarrel breaks out over who owns a particular prize marble. John gives me a Chinese burn. I bite his arm. Our mother runs in from the kitchen. John is told to go and play outside. I am taken through to the bathroom where my father's razor strop hangs on the wall …

From the hall I can either go into the sitting room on my left, or my parents' bedroom on my right. Or I can just keep going, launching myself down the steps and onto the glassed-in veranda. Since the chances are I'll find my father there, this is what I do. And there he is, sitting in his favourite high-backed chair, smoking his pipe. He's reading *The Outlook*, the weekly journal of the Presbyterian Church, but he drops it the moment I catapult into the room and grins at me. 'Dinner ready then, Nookie?' he says.

Happiness washes over me like rain. I could stay in this room forever, I think, as I explain that dinner's a wee way off yet but I've done my chores so here I am. I sit down at the long wooden table and rest my elbows in the spaces between my father's tobacco tin, his Zigzag tissues for his cigarettes, the large ashtray which it is my job to empty, and his box of matches. My father has called me 'Nook' or 'Nookie' for as long as I can remember. Not once have I heard him call me 'Elspeth'. It will be many years before I discover the other meaning of the word 'nookie', but by then it makes no difference. 'Nook' is still my family name, the one that triggers feelings of home. Only my mother called me Elspeth (though she had other names for me too; ones she took care my father never heard).

What do my father and I talk about? If I can't remember it's because it wasn't the *what* of our talk that mattered, it was the *how*. We talked as if we'd known each other for centuries and there was no need of words. Sometimes we sang. My father's repertoire was small, the words largely incomprehensible to me, but that was hardly a barrier. 'Again and again and again … My wife she died and I laughed and I cried …' If there was irony behind his choice of song – it was the one he sang or whistled more often than any other – I was blissfully unaware of it.

Since my mother has not yet called us to dinner (the main meal was eaten in the middle of the day) I take the chance to go through to the sitting room and do some piano practice. I'm still young enough to believe that my enthusiasm for the piano will take me, in just a few more years, to the concert halls of my fantasies. I've only ever been to one concert, to hear Solomon play on the grand piano in the Dunedin Town Hall, but it made such an impression on me I made up my mind there and then to become a concert pianist. My cousin Tom, who took me to that life-changing concert, was himself a talented pianist. With the illogic that informed much of my childhood thinking, I decided I had inherited his talent. It was only a matter of time before I too played in the town hall, and my mother, seated where I could see her, beamed with pride and clapped till her hands hurt.

I have to blow on my fingers before I can start playing. Lauriston is a cold house. On particularly bitter days I have to soak my hands in warm water to get my fingers to work. I think of the piano as mine, but in fact my mother plays too, not very often, and only because she needs to 'work' her fingers to stop them getting stiff. I can see her now, her arthritic hands hovering over the keys, singing softly as she plays 'Drink to Me Only', 'Sweet Molly Malone', 'Bring Back My Bonny', 'My Grandfather's Clock'. Did I know how much it hurt her to play? Was I aware of the pain that caused her to wince and bite her lip? Not that she ever let that stop her. Having set out to play for half an hour, that is what she would do, while I watched in awe, singing with her, hoping to catch an involuntary smile.

In time I will learn about my mother's Irish family, the Alleys, and her stories, like my father's, will become mine, but back then, listening to her singing, I'm filled with a longing as fierce as Uncle Vanya's or Count Orsino's. It's not what's in the songs I'm longing for, but what's in the singer. I long for my mother to love me.

On top of the piano is a photo of a favourite cousin of my father's. Her name is Sally Isherwood. She has shoulder-length curly hair which, to my child's eyes, means she is beautiful. My own hair is straight and fine, pulled into place each morning and fastened with a rubber band by my mother, with the addition, on Sundays, of a ribbon. My mother has instilled in me how plain I am. Pretty girls have curly hair. Plain girls look like me. The day I absorb the fact that my mother is not my mother I immediately assign that role to Sally. Someone at some time must have remarked on the similarity in our looks – or maybe that's something I imagined. However it came about, I clung to the belief that I was Sally Isherwood's daughter for the best part of two decades. It meant – and I see now that this was the key thing, not similarities, imagined or otherwise – that I was part of the Somerville family, for real. As for the identity of my birth father, of course I knew it didn't stack up, but I so badly wanted it to be true that I invented a past in which the man I called 'Pop' and Sally loved each other, but because they were cousins they couldn't marry. (Years later I would stumble on the exact same story, only the lover in question was not my father, it was my cousin, Jack. Had I heard this story before, when I was too young to understand it? As I was a compulsive eavesdropper it's more than likely.) How I came into the world – the word 'affair' would have meant nothing to me – didn't concern me. So long as I could tell myself my father had something to do with it, I was happy.

I'm still in the sitting room but it's filling up now with family. Saturday night is canasta night. My brother (John and I are allowed to stay up an hour later on Saturdays) is lying on the sofa. He has 'growing pains'. My mother is taking tender care of him. My father has lit the fire, using old copies of the *Otago Daily Times*, held over the fireplace, to coax the flames into life. Aunt Bessie, my father's sister, who 'kept house' for him during the long years of his bachelorhood, has walked across the paddocks from her bungalow, Braeside, smallest of the quartet of Somerville homes (Gladsmuir, Charlesfield and Lauriston being the other three), built within walking distance of the main house. Aunt Bessie and my mother don't like each other. Did I know that when I was a child? I don't think I did. But I understand now why Aunt Bessie befriended me, the cuckoo in the nest my mother had created for her husband and son. When my father married my mother, Aunt Bessie had to move out of Lauriston, the home she, like my father, had lived in all her life. The fact that her place was taken by an Irish woman from a family of known socialists (and worse!), with a history of suicide and mental breakdown, only added insult to injury. It would be many years before I heard the story of my Alley grandmother's tragic end, but Aunt Bessie made sure I knew about my Alley grandfather. 'He committed suicide, dear. Don't let them tell you it was an accident. He drove that poor horse over the cliff. And good riddance to bad rubbish I say. The man was a monster.'

Aunt Bessie is sitting opposite my father in the chair closest to the fire. I can see her scalp through her thin hair. She's wearing a shapeless navy frock that does nothing to disguise her capacious bosom. Watching her chest rise and fall I try to imagine what's under that unlovely frock. The picture that forms in my mind is of a small black and white dog, nestling in the warmth of her bosom, breathing in and out, as Aunt Bessie chats about her Sunday School pupils and the baking she will be doing for the next Sunday School picnic.

My mother has prepared a competitive supper. Aunt Bessie is famous for her date scones and her fruit cake, so my mother, not to be outdone, has baked a sponge cake filled with raspberry jam, and my father's favourite sultana biscuits. Now someone else is arriving – Uncle Jim from Gladsmuir, my father's younger brother and business partner (my father is the chairman, my uncle a director of Coulls Somerville Wilkie, forerunner of present-day Whitcoulls). Uncle Jim has a dashing moustache and seven grown-up children. I love him almost as much as I love my father. Something happens to the room as he enters it. It's as if there's suddenly more air and more warmth. My father laughs out loud. He has a distinctive laugh, culminating in a snort, which invariably makes everyone else laugh. Aunt Bessie giggles. I'm standing behind my father's chair, giddy with happiness.

As soon as the three of them are seated around the card table (my mother doesn't play) the game begins. It's not always canasta. Some evenings they play cribbage, shouting out strange rhymes – 'fifteen two, fifteen four …' – that I store away along with abracadabra and other magic formulas ('She loves me, she loves me not …'). Aunt Bessie cheats. Her brothers must be aware of this but they don't say anything. From time to time my father gets up to put another log on the fire. Now the warmth in the room has reached the bay windows on the far side. Surely my brother doesn't need that eiderdown my mother has just fetched for him.

When the game ends, with Aunt Bessie the inevitable winner, mention is made of Uncle Harry Renfree who, since the death of his wife Minnie, my father's older sister, has lived with Bessie. Men, it seems, cannot live on their own.

I look across at my brother. Is Uncle Harry, whom we both fear, going to be walking across the paddocks to play canasta too? But no, Uncle Harry doesn't approve of cards, not even on weekdays.

My brother grins at me and winks. 'Big black bat,' he mouths.

I would like to stay in that room forever, with the fire blazing, the trolley laden with cakes, and, with a little adjustment of the card-playing scene, my mother at the piano singing 'Molly Malone'. But I know I have to look into the other room off the hallway, my parents' bedroom. It's not a room I go into if I can help it, not unless my father is there. Sunday nights, when my father goes to bed early, my brother and I are allowed to climb into bed with him. Hunkering down among the many pillows, listening to our father's gentle voice tell the story of Baby Moses in the bullrushes, or the vanquishing of the giant Goliath by the pint-sized David, turns the room, for a magical half hour, from a place of confusion and anxiety – I once tried to get into bed with my mother, a big mistake – into a place of enchantment. Sometimes the stories our father tells are not from the Bible but from his own and the family's past. I thought he was telling us everything that had happened in his life. Now of course I know he was telling us only the merest fraction.

Like the kitchen, the predominant colour in the bedroom is green (carpet, walls, eiderdowns), but this green is stronger, uncontaminated by smoke and coal dust. The room is large, with a wide expanse of carpet in the middle. I'm sure of this because I can count how many steps it takes to get from one bed to the other. That my parents slept as far apart from each other as possible seemed normal to me as a child. I remember the shock I experienced the day I first discovered that some parents actually shared a bed. How did that work? How did they manage to sleep, tucked up next to each other? By the time I discovered that some parents even took baths together I was a little more savvy about the facts of life, but there is a part of me that still thinks of Adam and Eve as polite strangers, not intimate bedfellows.

My own bedroom, at the far end of the corridor off the hall, has, like most of the rooms in the house, a fireplace with an empty grate. The colour I see is yellow, though I'm sure there were other colours as well. It's an odd, L-shaped room, as if part of it were once a box room, with sharp corners that I repeatedly walked into on my nighttime rambles. I don't know when my sleepwalking stopped – it was still going on, with embarrassing consequences, in my late teens – but I do remember the dreams that prompted it. The worst involved a bear that systematically ate first my father, then my mother, then my brother, finally turning to me, paralysed with fear, in the corner of the room. The other recurring dream featured a man pushing a wheelbarrow around the house. I've no idea what was in the wheelbarrow but I do remember the overpowering need to stop him going any further. What would happen if I failed in my mission was not clear, but I can still feel the terror that gripped me as I struggled to reach him.

Does this mean I was afraid of the dark? I can see myself checking under the bed for monsters, but I don't remember being frightened once I'd satisfied myself there was nothing lurking beneath the bedsprings. No, it was not the dark the frightened me, it was the light. To this day I prefer winter to summer. When I first experienced those long English nights, when the light starts to fail in the mid-afternoon, I felt I'd been given a gift. Safe behind drawn curtains, away from the searchlight sun, I could dream my way back to hopefulness.

It's cold in my bedroom. I undress under the blankets, shivering at the touch of the icy sheets, clutching the hot-water bottle with its knitted cover that my mother has filled for me. I can't rest my feet on the hottie because I have chilblains, and exposure to heat makes them itch. So I clutch it to my chest and bury my head under the blankets to block out the sounds from the wireless. Since the wireless is in the sitting room at the other end of the house, and the door is shut tight, I shouldn't be able to hear anything, but my father is deaf so the volume has been turned up. 4YC plays classical music, the kind I like, but there's something about hearing it at such a distance that leeches out joy. As I lie in my bed, arms tightly crossed to avoid the frosty margins, even a wild Hungarian dance sounds sad to my ears. I still puzzle about this – that music, which has been both inspiration and solace for the whole of my life, can at times be too much to bear.

Sometimes I am woken not by nightmares but by nose bleeds. I like it when this happens because my mother is kind to me. She takes me through to the kitchen, sits me by the coal range and puts a cold flannel on the back of my neck while she pinches the top of my nose to stop the bleeding. After it's over, she makes me a warm milk drink and finds me a fresh pyjama top. Occasionally the bleed is really bad and my father joins us in the kitchen, and more cold things – keys, ice blocks – are held against my neck. I feel woozy after the bad bleeds so my mother lets me have a biscuit, and puts honey into the warm drink. Eventually my father leads me back along the corridor, and stays with me till I fall asleep.

My brother's bedroom is some distance away, closer to my parents' room. I'm trying to see it but I can only visualise parts of it. We used to share a bedroom but this stopped when I was about seven. In the centre of the floor is his Meccano train set – I can see that clearly. And I can see the bookshelf with Arthur Mee's encyclopedias and the *Just William* and *Biggles* books. If I haven't already read *Biggles* I soon will. The girls' version – *Worrals* – is tame compared to the adventures that befall Biggles and his mate Ginger. As for the *Just William* books: I don't have to try at all to see my brother curled up in a chair, laughing his head off as he reads. Little wonder that, having read my way through Enid Blyton's *Anne of Green Gables*, *Black Beauty* and the stories (read to please my mother) of Nurse Sue Barton, that I turned my attention to the books on my brother's shelves. A preparatory foray, as it turned out, before tackling my father's library.

I'm in awe of my brother. He never makes my mother angry. How does he do that? And he's mischievous, far more than I would ever dare to be. He climbs hedges, right to the top. That's how he broke his arm, a break so bad he had to have steel plates put in. My mother said it was my fault, since we were playing together when it happened, but she was crying when she said it so I didn't get punished. I spent a lot of my childhood wishing I *was* my brother. He had thick black curls, which meant he was good-looking, and he didn't have to peel apples or wash dishes or clean out the hen-run. But mostly I wanted to be him so that my mother would like me. One spectacular Sunday, when he was supposed to be at Sunday School, he got behind the wheel of our father's car, let off the brake and hurtled all the way down Andersons Bay Road. People said it was a miracle he wasn't killed, but I knew it wasn't that – it was a sign of how clever he was. He was only six, but he knew all about cars and how they worked.

*****

Lauriston has five bedrooms, all, at least in memory, large and cold, with windows that rattle in the wind, and pictures of faraway places on the walls. Jerusalem and the Sea of Galilee feature prominently, as does St Andrew's University, where my clerical cousins went to study theology. Hanging in one of the spare bedrooms is a large painting of Glencoe, where the Campbells, to whom the Somervilles are connected (my brother was christened John Campbell Somerville) massacred the MacDonalds.

The two spare bedrooms are halfway up a corridor that leads to the coal store, the washhouse and the lavatory. On one memorable occasion my brother and his friend (possibly our cousin Alan, now a well-known sculptor based in Sydney) managed to lock the lavatory door from the outside while I was inside. 'Oh dear, what can the matter be / Three old maids all locked in the lavatory / They were there from Monday to Saturday / Nobody knew they were there.' I imagine I screamed, though I don't remember doing so. Practical jokes are part and parcel of Somerville family tradition. Screaming would have been bad form.

Further down the corridor, nearer to the rest of the house, is the bathroom, cold and yellow and, for me, a place of complex significance. It's in this room, just before I start school, that my mother tells me I'm adopted. I see her now, on her knees beside the bath, a tin of Chemico in her hand, the inevitable apron obscuring her dress, a look on her face I don't remember ever seeing before. I'm tempted to say she's smiling but I don't think she is; just looking at me as if she cares about me. 'If anyone at school ever tries to tell you you're not ours,' she says, 'then you must tell them they're wrong. You're ours far more than most children because your father and I chose you. Other mothers and fathers have to take what comes along, but you and your brother were chosen, so you're special.'

It takes a long time for the meaning of those words to sink in. I'm too mesmerised by the look in my mother's eyes. She loves me, that's the message I take from the bathroom that day. She chose *me* out of millions of babies. In my mind I see a long room stretching into the distance, filled with bassinets and babies. My father and mother are walking down the room peering into the bassinets, shaking their heads, till they reach the one with me in it. They stop, peer, look at each other, and nod. I kick my legs and laugh out loud. I am The Chosen One. I'm special.

But the bathroom holds another memory, one I'm far less keen to revisit. My brother and I are having a bath together. The bathroom is a long way from the sitting room, where our parents are listening to the wireless. John has just turned six. I am four. Despite Truby King's exhortation to bathe daily we only have two baths a week. It's wartime and hot water is rationed, at least in our household. So John and I sit in three inches of tepid water in the middle of winter, oblivious to the cold, thrilled to have been left unsupervised. We float our boats – John's is an aircraft carrier, mine is a destroyer – on the soapy scum. Our flannels are filled with air and blown up to make islands, around which our boats, pursued by enemy submarines, are forced to navigate. 'You're barmy you're barmy your mother's in the army …' In between zooming in for the kill, we belt out the words of the song we've been forbidden to sing.

Suddenly my brother does a wildly daring thing. He turns on the taps.

'What are you doing?' I gasp.

'Making an ocean,' he answers.

'But we're not allowed,' I protest.

'Don't worry. Mum won't come. She's listening to her programme.'

'But we'll get into trouble,' I say, though what I mean is, *I'll* get into trouble.

'I'm not scared.'

'Me not either,' I agree, determined to match my brother's courage.

When John clambers out of the bath, I follow him. The linoleum feels slippery under my feet. The noise of the running water is exhilarating. As I wait for the bath to fill my heart turns somersaults in my chest. This is the most exciting thing that has ever happened to me. When the water reaches the top I look at John. Surely he'll turn the taps off now? But he doesn't 'Look!' he says. 'A waterfall.'

The water slops onto my toes. 'Turn off!' I shout, courage deserting me as suddenly as it arrived. 'Turn off!'

'Wheeee …!' John shouts, as his boat sloshes onto the floor. 'It's the Niagara Falls. Come on Nook, your turn!'

The door opens. My mother looms in the doorway. She looks as if she's about to turn into a pillar of stone. For the longest moment she neither moves nor speaks. Then she erupts into action, pushing past us, turning off the taps and pulling out the plug. By this time I'm shivering all over.

'Run!' John hisses as he slithers past me. 'Hide!'

But I'm paralysed. My feet are stuck to the linoleum, my back is pressed against the wall. As John vanishes I try to make myself invisible. If Alice in Wonderland could do it, why can't I?

My mother throws a towel onto the floor and turns to the basin. I see her hand on the razor strop and I know what's coming. Instinctively I raise my hands to cover my face. Most of the hidings she has given me have hurt my hands and legs, but this is not like those times, this is different. Her face is blotchy. Her eyes are black.

'No, Alice, no!'

It's my father, appearing like the angel Gabriel, in the doorway. My mother never uses the strap on me when my father is around, so how did he know what was going to happen? I look at him, but what I see – a man with tears in his eyes – frightens me far more than my mother's rage, so I do what my brother told me to do and run. Where I end up is in the broom cupboard in the porch. It smells of boot polish and Jeyes Fluid. The bristles on the brooms tickle my backside. I sneeze, and my hiding place is discovered. But I don't get the strap. My mother, her voice bitter as lemons, tells my father it's his job to discipline me. 'She will have put him up to it, you can be sure,' she says.

'Very well, dear,' my father answers. 'But first let's find her pyjamas and get her warmed up. She'll catch her death out here.'

I don't remember how the evening ended. I wasn't punished. Neither was my brother. But that was the last time we bathed together.

*****

The last room on my tour of the house is in many ways the most mysterious. Known as the breakfast room, it was the scene of family Christmases when upwards of twenty people would sit around the expanded table, and the crockery and crystal hidden away in mahogany sideboards and glass-fronted cabinets, and the embroidered linen which my mother would have starched to a crisp, snow-whiteness, would make their annual appearance, drawing words of admiration from the many uncles and aunts and cousins who looked on Lauriston as home. Walking into that room on any other day was like walking into church. You held your breath for fear of doing or saying the wrong thing. Perhaps that's why my brother and I tended to avoid it. Though I could never quite resist the attraction of the padlocked trunk, and the roll-top desk with the hollowed out space for the inkwell and the rows of drawers, two of which were permanently locked. Once the realisation that my brother and I were different from other children had sunk in, I became convinced that what lay behind those locks were secrets about the two of us. If only I could find the key!

Decades later, at a family reunion, I was given the family Bible that had belonged to my father. For months I didn't bother to look at it. It was large and heavy, the kind of object used to flatten carbuncles. But one day I started to flick through the tissue-thin pages and there, at the beginning of Jeremiah, were these words: 'Look under the third floorboard of Grandma's death room.' A quick call to cousin Jack established that Grandma's death room was in fact the breakfast room. A further call to the current owners of Lauriston – the serendipitously named Mr and Mrs Angel – revealed that the room had been carpeted, and the Angels, understandably, unwilling to pull the carpet up. So the mystery remains. My childhood self would have woven a tale of lost love and treasure. My adult self, sobered by the knowledge of who the Somervilles were and are, is convinced that what lies under that third floorboard is Grandma Marion's thoughts on how to earn yourself a place in heaven. 'Be Good Sweet Maid and Let Who Will be Clever.' 'Cleanliness is Next to Godliness'. 'Do Good and Serve the Lord.' 'In My Father's House are Many Mansions.'

Laying up treasure on earth was never the Somerville way.

Chapter Nineteen

'The past is not dead. It's not even past.'
William Faulkner

'**Places belong** to the people who love them,' Margaret Atwood has claimed. So Lauriston, more than any other place I have lived in, belongs to me. Which doesn't mean it was a happy place, though intermittently it was. Rather it was a place that seemed to contain everything, not just what I was to become 'for better or worse', but a vision, in microcosm, of what life is. None of which, of course, was clear to me at the time. I didn't need Kierkegaard to tell me that we live life forwards, but understand it backwards. That had always seemed obvious to me. So I understand now why I sometimes wanted to run away from the place I loved so deeply.

The shadow of my mother's complex feelings about me – there would be times, after she fell ill, when I was the only person she would allow near her – kept menacing company with my own shadow, so that sometimes the need to escape overwhelmed me. But dreaming of flight is one thing, putting it into practice is another. The only time I crept out the door intent on never coming back I was found – hiding in my hut in the macrocarpa hedge – not by my mother, whom I had wanted to punish, but by my father. It was dusk and I was beginning to regret my foolhardiness. It was one thing to hide out in my hut, where I had previously secreted a packet of ginger biscuits and a stash of apples from the orchard, but quite another to hold out until the day after, and the day after that. When I heard my father's voice calling my name I didn't hesitate. I threw myself out through the branches and ran into his arms. That was when I saw he was crying. The realisation that instead of punishing my mother I had caused my father to cry crushed whatever remained of my self-pity. 'Sorry sorry, I'm so so sorry, please don't cry, Poppity, please.'

Nothing was said when we got back to the house. I was given a cup of Ovaltine and sent to bed. While my father was alive I would never run away again.

*****

If the Jesuits are right, and it's in the first seven year of life that a person's character is formed, then Lauriston must have left its mark on several generations of Somervilles. I find this notion comforting. It means that, despite my genetic difference, I have been shaped by the same cold corridors and draughty rooms, the same high hedges and abundant gardens, the same rough paddocks and forbidden fruit trees, as my father, my uncles and aunts, and the many cousins who came and went, like migrating birds returning to the source of food and warmth.

But for all the sturdy reassurance it offered, Lauriston, like every other home in the land, could not escape the shadow of war. By the time we left – a move ostensibly triggered by my father's inability to navigate the long, steep driveway – the war had been over for six years. But that in no way diminished its influence. Everything I understood about the world outside of my family came from what I had pieced together, thanks to my eavesdropping skills, about the war. I never doubted for a moment that it had been a monumental struggle between good and evil, and that good – people like me, white-skinned and Presbyterian – had won. The Japanese killed my missionary uncle; the Germans murdered the Jews. Several years would pass before other truths – Dresden, Hiroshima, the crimes committed (by people like me) on the indigenous populations of the colonised world – shifted my view of that war and the essential division between good people and bad, good nations and bad.

Driving across the causeway one day I asked my father about the boarded-up cave in the hillside ahead of us. The war had been over for several years but the army notice prohibiting entry was still nailed across the entrance. 'Why?' I asked. 'What's in there? Guns?'

'I doubt it,' my father answered. 'Not any more. But you're on the right track, Nookie. It was almost certainly used to store weapons during the war.'

'Don't you know?'

'I'm not in the army, Sweetheart.'

'Perhaps it was a hiding place. Like our air-raid shelter.'

'It may well have become that,' my father replied, the smile gone from his voice now, 'if the Japs had invaded.'

I never did get to see inside that cave. When I learned, years later, that Maori prisoners, guilty of nothing more than peaceful protest, had been held captive there in the late nineteenth century, chained to its walls for months at a time, I felt, as I have since in earthquakes, as if the ground under my feet was no longer solid. I had walked past the cave so many times, imagining deeds of wartime heroism involving myself and my brother, innocent of the horror written on its walls. Now I had to peel away those memories and look at the uncomfortable truth that 'people like me' had locked up people who were different, for the 'crime' of resisting the forced appropriation of their lands. The word confiscation, which till then I had associated with Nazi crimes against the Jews, suddenly had relevance much closer to home.

'Hate the sin but not the sinner,' I'd heard my father say.

'So you don't hate Hitler?' someone – my Uncle Jim, I think (I was eavesdropping again) – answered him.

'No, I pity him.'

*****

But it was not pity that brought two English girls, refugees from the Blitz, to live on the Otago Peninsula. It was fear. Moira and Catherine were sisters, nieces of my mother's nursing friend, 'Auntie Connie'. (Friends of my parents who had anything to do with my brother and me had aunt or uncle status automatically conferred on them.) Transported 12,000 miles to escape the German bombs, they were a direct link to the mysterious families my mother sent food parcels to. I imagined other children who spoke and dressed like them (tailored skirts; 'Pringle' twinsets) opening parcels from Lauriston, exclaiming in delight over the tins of dripping, condensed milk, Ovaltine, golden syrup, peas; the packets of cocoa, milk powder, biscuits, tea; plus, the prize at the heart of it all, my mother's home-baked fruit cake wrapped in muslin. My mother had explained that the parcels were going to families in the 'East End', but since I had no idea where that was, other than that it was in London, the picture in my mind was still of Moira and Catherine lookalikes, oohing and aahing over the goodies from New Zealand. No one told me it was only the upper classes who could afford to send their children out of the country. Even if I had been told, I would not have understood. I had to wait till I went to England myself to fully grasp the meaning of that ordinary little word, *class*.

As regular visitors to Lauriston, Moira and Catherine were more like cousins than visitors from a faraway land. The woman acting as their mother was, after all, an auntie. Surely that made them cousins? I don't know whether it was the way they talked (as if their father were the king) or the fact of their being older that accounted for my devotion to them. I only know I followed them around like Mary's little lamb, hanging on to their every word, dizzy with happiness when they took more than passing notice of me.

Every spring they would come to help my brother and me pick the daffodils that grew in such profusion on the slope behind the henhouse. I'm not sure if I remember these annual events as I would have been under five, but I have a photo of the four of us, our arms filled with daffodils, Moira and Catherine in their neat English clothes, my brother wearing his trusty tin helmet, and me in a kilt looking annoyed. What I do remember is the day Moira and Catherine *didn't* come to pick daffodils. It would have been the spring of 1945. 'What's happened to them?' I asked John. 'Has someone kidnapped them?'

'Don't be a drongo.'

'Well, why aren't they here?'

'It's not right,' I heard my mother say to Auntie Connie, who'd come on her own to help with the harvest. (The flowers were destined for the city's hospitals. Auntie Connie, matron of the hospital where my mother had once nursed, invariably went away with the lion's share.) 'Their father killed. Their house bombed out. Living in a city where the queues stretch halfway around the block. They should have stayed with you till things were back to normal.'

'At least I had them for a while,' Auntie Connie replied. 'Really I should be grateful to the Germans.'

'Where have they gone?' I asked my mother later.

'Home,' she replied, the word slipping out between tight lips.

Did she give the word a capital H as my father did? What did an Irish woman, imbued with the sternest form of Christianity and a messianic view of how the world should be governed, think of England and the Empire? Not a lot she could share with her Somerville in-laws, I suspect.

*****

I attribute to Lauriston my acute sensitivity to houses. There are buildings I can hardly bear to enter, so powerful is the feeling that something is not right within their walls. My aversion, three and a half decades later, to the house Maurice Shadbolt asked me to share with him in Titirangi, owes a lot to this hyper-sensitivity (though the house, which I secretly labelled after my first visit a health hazard, was hardly a lovers' dream). It's still not something I can explain rationally. It's a paradox that Lauriston, where things happened that I shrink from in memory even now, continues to exert this hold on me, but I believe it is at least partly explained by the sheer number of escape routes it provided. Long before I started school I discovered the solace of being on my own, a gift that would later fuel my life as a writer. It was said of Woody Guthrie that he wrote – songs, poems, novels – out of a yearning for release and escape. For the first eleven years of my life I didn't need to write; I had Lauriston. Once I no longer had that refuge, I found another way to escape.

'Tara! Home! I'll go home,' Scarlett O'Hara shouts, when everything else in her life has failed. I can't go back physically to the Lauriston of my childhood, but I can, and do, go back in imagination. It is my hiding place.

*****

It's time to take leave of Lauriston. I close my eyes, and the face I see is my father's. I hear him whistling in the garden; catch him waving from behind the wheel of his big brown Plymouth while my brother and I try to jump on the running-board; glimpse him through the sitting-room window playing patience at the green baize card table. Then I see him coming through the door after a day visiting the pulp and paper mills of which he is a director, at Mataura, his head swathed in a bandage – one of two occasions when he drove the Plymouth into the Clutha River and lived to tell the tale. (My father learned to drive before licences were issued, and continued to drive as if his was the only car on the road.) I see him positioning his hat on his bald head, whistling cheerfully as he sets out to visit the sick, as if he were the minister, not merely the session clerk, of the Andersons Bay Presbyterian Church. I see him locked in earnest conversation with Robbie, our gardener, whose dispensing of tobacco-flecked blackballs to my brother and me we kept secret from our health-obsessed mother. I see him at the head of the table on Christmas Day 1944, almost my earliest memory. Twenty-five people are seated around that table. Thousands of peas have been shelled, dozens of new potatoes scrubbed. Four huge legs of lamb have been roasting since dawn. Now it is time for the Christmas pudding to be dished up, for the wedding ring to arrive mysteriously on the plate of 'Maori Hill Bill', the family's perennial bachelor, and for threepences to appear by the same alchemy on the plates of the many children. My father stands and proposes a toast. Glasses filled with cordial (this is a teetotal house) are raised. We drink to peace, and to the safe return of Padre Jack and Cousin Tom, the two soldiers in the family. Finally I see my father in the house we moved to after we left Lauriston, on his knees (Presbyterians at that time were resolute non-kneelers), his shoulders heaving as the burden of his wife's mental illness, and the horror of what might lie ahead for the two cuckoos in his nest, sinks home. Four months after my fourteenth birthday he is dead.

My Alley grandparents. After the suicide of my grandmother Alice, my grandfather, Henry, remarried and had twelve more children.

The grave of my grandmother, Alice Alley, and the two babies who drowned with her.

Ken Tompkins, my birth father, taken in the mid-1920s. The woman in the car is his sister-in-law, Marjorie, Lance Tompkins' wife.

Above: Ken Tompkins (on right) in 1929 with Skip Barnes and Bob Murie. The three were placegetters in the first New Zealand ski championship. Graham Collection, from Alan C. Graham, *Mount Ruapehu: 100 years of skiing, Balasoglou Books, 2013.*

Left: Lance Tompkins, my father's brother.

Below: My birth mother in her early twenties.

*Alice Alley, my adoptive mother,
as a young nurse.*

*Jim and Grace Somerville, beloved uncle
and aunt.*

*Tom and
Alice
Somerville,
my adoptive
parents,
on their
wedding
day.*

Above: The Truby King Harris Karitane Hospital where I spent the first nine months of my life.

Facing page: Photos take by Nurse Margaret Dunlop the day I left the Truby King Hospital to begin life with my adoptive family. My name was changed from Nan to Elspeth. (The dates at the top are wrong!)

Truby King Harris Hospital, Andersons Bay, c/nE4928/14, Hocken Collections]

"Nan"
at
Karitane
1939-40

In General Ward with
Plunket Nurses.

The day "Nan"
went home.

Above: At top, Lauriston, the Somerville family home, where I spent the first decade of my life. Lauriston was known in the family as Up By, with the original Somerville home, Charlesfield (at base of hill), known as Down By. Left: A pre-First World War photo of Lauriston.

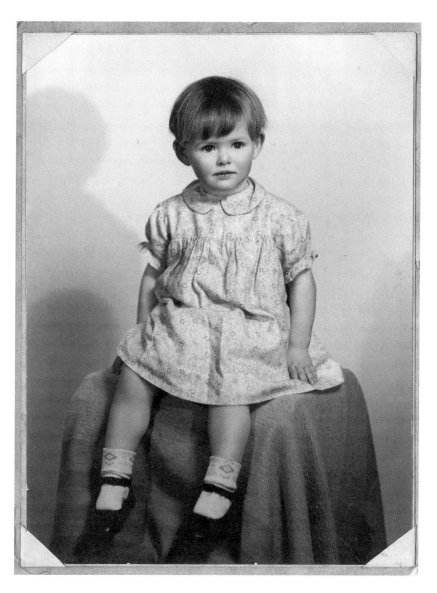

I have no memory of this photo being taken but I seem to remember the dress.

Facing page, clockwise from top left: In costume for the Otago Centennial pageant in 1948;

With my brother John;

The entrance to 234 Musselburgh Rise;

Tom and Alice on my father's eightieth birthday, in the garden of 234 Musselburgh Rise.

Above: Daffodil Day at Lauriston, with Catherine and Moira, refugees from England.

Below: Lauriston family Christmas, 1942 or 43. My father holding me (right), my mother directly behind. Uncle Jim and Aunt Grace seated at the left. Terrifying Aunt Jim (Jemima) sitting in the centre. The others are all cousins.

At the top of the Crown Range on one of our Wanaka holidays.

Above: Rewi Alley on one of his early visits to New Zealand, with his sisters Joy and Gwen.

In my Columba College uniform with my parents soon after we moved to 234.

At 234 again, aged fourteen.

Right: Debutantes: with Fay Smith in the garden of 234.

Left: Charles and Betty Smith with younger daughter Ann in the garden of their home, early 1950s.

Above: Jack and Janet Somerville at Jack's investiture into the Order of New Zealand.

Left: Cousin Jack in wartime.

Above: Margot and Angus Ross, and Margot's daughter Jocelyn, in the garden of their home in Alison Crescent.

Left: Margot and Angus Ross at the time of their marriage, in the garden of Alison Crescent.

Below: Miss Buchan, principal of Columba College.

Top: A school photo of my birth mother, Betty.

Above: With Jennie Blakeney, my oldest friend, at a Bible Class camp.

Facing page: My birth mother, Betty, in her Invercargill garden with her husband Ken Gray (right).

My father relaxing at the Wanaka Lodge.

My birth father, Ken Tompkins (right), with his wife Patricia next to him, and their son Tony, my half-brother, next to her. His wife Diana is in the red dress, and the others are their children and friends. Taken two years before my meeting with my father.

Chapter Twenty

'O! let me not be mad, not mad, sweet heaven ...'
WILLIAM SHAKESPEARE

I don't remember the day we moved out of Lauriston. I was eleven years old. If, as is often claimed, we are what we remember, then this gap in my store of memories is significant. I suspect my efficient mother managed the whole thing with minimal disruption to my father's routine, but I'm surprised I don't remember panic or stress, or being punished for daydreaming when I was supposed to be cleaning out drawers or hanging out the washing. Now that I know the illness that had already begun to afflict my mother was mental not physical, I can imagine a narrative in which she manages the entire move to our new home during one of her manic periods. Later would come complete collapse, far more terrifying to me than the whirlwinds she created when she was on a 'high'. But at the time of the move this pattern – mania followed by clinical depression – had not been fully established. Her long absence in hospital, a year or so before the move, had been downplayed as some kind of medical misadventure. The story my brother and I were told was that she'd been given the wrong drugs. 'Sulphur,' Aunt Bessie informed us, tapping the side of her nose. 'Turns out she's allergic.'

None of which explains why I have wiped all knowledge of the move from my memory. I loved Lauriston. Surely I would have felt *something* the day we left it for good. The only explanation I can come up with is one I have difficulty coming to terms with. I was pretending to be happy about moving, faking an emotion in order to please my mother. That I would go on doing this, in one form or another, in my adult life is not something I am proud of. Because the problem with pretending, at least in childhood, is that too often you are unaware you are doing it. Later, when my mother, psychologically speaking, was replaced by whatever man I was

117

currently involved with, I would repeat this pattern, agreeing to things I would later come to resent, in order to keep the peace. That this was grossly unfair to the man in question is something I acknowledge now with sorrow and regret. Failing to make my wishes known simply paved the way for subsequent disenchantment. Like most women of my generation I eagerly embraced feminism when it came along, but it's hard, in retrospect, to see myself as a feminist when I was so busy sacrificing what I wanted simply to avoid conflict.

(I'm reminded of Janet Malcolm's assertion that all autobiography is 'an exercise in self-forgiveness'. Is that what I'm doing here? Forgiving myself for a lifetime of trying to please others?)

There is, of course, another much simpler explanation for why I have forgotten the day of the move: I was excited about our new home. 234 Musselburgh Rise was a far grander house than Lauriston. Built in the nineteenth century by the eponymous James Anderson (Andersons Bay), the house boasted five bedrooms, a breakfast/dining room, a drawing room (used only on the rarest of occasions), a music room (also known as the billiard room), a double-sided, glassed-in veranda, a butler's pantry, a wine cellar, laundry, coalhouse, bathroom and kitchen. The corridor was long enough for John and me to commandeer it to play indoor hockey. At its far end there were three steps leading to the drawing room, music room and sunroom (veranda). When my mother was in a benign mood she would let me stage plays, using the corridor as the stage, with the audience seated in the hallway, no doubt in a terrible draught. Perhaps not surprisingly, given the content of my father's library, all the plays I chose had their origins in English or Scottish history. The one I remember best was about the Civil War: a roundhead soldier in love with the daughter of a cavalier general. Needless to say I cast myself as the heroine, while my reluctant brother mumbled his way through the part of the hero.

*****

If the move to 234 was, as I had been told, to make life easier for my father, it must have had the opposite effect on my mother. She had simply replaced one unreconstructed nineteenth-century house with another, larger version. The only concessions to the modern world were the electric stove in the kitchen, and the primitive washing machine in the laundry. Otherwise it was business as usual: looking after my father; dealing with the various women who came to help and invariably failed to meet her high standards, coping (God knows how) with her own unstable mental condition.

As for the surrounds, they were as grand as the house itself – landscaped gardens; a gold fish pond; two greenhouses; two garages; an entire stable, complete with hay loft and stalls; a henhouse; several sheds; a colonial cottage built by James Anderson to house his family while the main house was being built. With more than two acres of garden, plus a patch of bush where, to my sorrowful delight, I discovered soon after we moved a stone slab with the words 'GAVIN BEST DOG IN THE WORLD DIED JULY 14 1923' etched on it, I should have been able to map out escape routes similar to those I had relied on at Lauriston. But though there were places I could go to where I felt safe – the stable loft being favourite – I never succeeded in creating an alternative universe for myself as I had at Lauriston. It was as if, to the shadow of my mother's complex feelings about me, was now added what I was learning about her illness, information gleaned from conversations with her psychiatrist Dr Medlicott, who treated her when she became a patient at Ashburn Hall, the private psychiatric hospital of which he was superintendent. I don't remember anyone else ever talking seriously to me about what was wrong with her. Throwaway remarks and the occasional jibe were the only indications I had that the subject was being discussed at all. As for the sulphur drug story, I suspect that was simply the family's way of dealing with the elephant in the room. But grateful though I was for Dr Medlicottt's gentle explanations, they did little to prepare me for what was to come.

One of the first things I did after we moved to 234 was spend all my pocket money buying a horse destined for the knackers' yard, an action that aroused my tender-hearted father to a rare display of irritation (the horse had to be returned; my five pounds was not). How I knew this poor old nag was about to be put out of his misery I can't now remember. But the grief and outrage I experienced as I watched the condemned horse being taken away was not so easily forgotten. My friend Jennie and I had lovingly prepared one of the stalls in the stable, buying hay and oats in preparation for the horse's arrival, resurrecting a halter and bridle found hanging in the tack room, but none of this cut any ice with my parents. The horse was gone before he'd had time to finish his first feed of oats.

*****

234 is where my father died. Perhaps that's the reason I don't keep returning to its chilly rooms and outdoor hiding places, as I do with Lauriston. When I think of 234 now what I feel is panic, and a sense, already implanted, but stronger than ever after my father's death, of entrapment.

I close my eyes and what I see is my thirteen-year-old self, walking up the drive that leads from the street, past the safety of the neighbours' houses, to reach the gate that leads into the back of 234. It's night. I've been to a school concert. Or perhaps to a Bible Class dance. I go through the gate and it's suddenly dark. To my right is a narrow stretch of bush; to my left, the stable, looming above me like a medieval tower. No horses shelter there, so the murmurings and whisperings I hear all around me are not their doing. Something is alive in that densely dark patch of bush. What, or who, is it? The henhouse is further up the drive, close to the house. But I know the noises hens make, and what I am hearing is nothing like. My feet crunch on the gravel. My father's car, parked in one of the two garages, glows in the pale moonlight. It's not a car but a ghostly chariot. 'Like one that on a lonesome road/ Doth walk in fear and dread ...' I've recently learned Coleridge's 'Ancient Mariner' by heart. I wish I hadn't. 'Because he knows a frightful fiend/ Doth close behind him tread ...'

By the time I reach the house I'm out of breath. I've walked slowly so as not to disturb whatever is lurking in the bush, but I'm gasping for air as if I've just climbed a mountain. I open the door. The light is dim. It comes from the laundry. I should turn it off – that's the rule – but if I do the whole house will be in darkness.

I tiptoe down the corridor. The door to my parents' room is shut. As is the door to the sitting room. The wireless is silent. My brother, who sleeps at the other end of the house, is either out, or doing the mysterious things he does these days behind his own closed door.

I reach my bedroom and shut the door. Now the only sound is from the ventilator in the ceiling. I sit on my narrow bed and listen to what I tell myself is the breath of God. But I'm not comforted by the thought. My father is slowly disappearing. Every day there seems to be less of him. While my mother, from whose illness he has shielded us for so long, looms over every minute of the day, as if to punish time for what is about to happen.

*****

As I remember it, my mother's first really bad bout of depression occurred soon after we moved. I came home from school (I would have been in my last year at Andersons Bay Primary) to find her still in her dressing gown – an unthinkable departure from the norm – curled in the foetal position in the corner of her bedroom. It was to be the first of many such discoveries. Where was my father at these times? He was still a director of a number of companies, and session clerk of the Andersons Bay Church, so I imagine he was at a meeting. After a while I became used to finding my mother this way, but that first time was deeply shocking. I picked her up, got her into bed, and made her a cup of tea. She didn't speak – she barely looked at me – but she did drink the tea. I imagine I told my father about it when he came home, but what was said or done has been overshadowed by what followed.

The next time I arrived home to find my mother in that state (it could even have been the following day) she asked me, once I'd got her into bed, to get in beside her. I don't know what I said – naturally I obeyed her – but I've no doubt the shock I was feeling was written on my face. I'd long ago given up hope of ever being asked to get into bed with her. What was I to do? Should I cuddle her? Kiss her? Lie still without touching? Whatever I did was obviously acceptable, because she started talking straight away. I don't remember how much was said on that first occasion – there would be many more – but over the course of those few weeks, till the ambulance came to take her to Ashburn Hall, I learned things about her that would haunt me for the rest of my life. Sometimes she just lay beside me quietly moaning, but at other times she would talk as if desperate to get the story of her unhappy life out of her system.

While she was still alive I never told anyone the things she told me. Her father, whom I had met only once – a terrifying Old Testament figure with a long beard and a bony, sharp-edged body – was a frightening enough memory even then for me to believe every word she told me about his harshness as a parent, and the cruel indifference with which he dragged his new young bride (my mother's mother, a music teacher with no experience of farm life) from one remote piece of bush to another. Hacking out pasture from the wilderness was his passion. As soon as a farm became viable (and sellable) he bought another section of bush and set about with axe and spade and saw to create something from nothing. And all the time the babies kept coming, one a year, till on an otherwise unremarkable morning in 1897 my grandmother took her six children (my mother being the second-eldest) to the river and attempted to drown them all. The four older children escaped. The two babies – three-week-old Rose and 18-month-old Lucy – died with their mother. Alice, my mother, named for her mother, was seven years old.

I never did find out how much my father knew of my mother's blighted childhood. She told me her story in fits and starts, interspersing it with incidents from her nursing days and other disconnected memories from her past. I don't think I fully grasped the tragedy of what had happened to her till I was an adult living 12,000 miles away. Dr Medlicott, in one of our conversations, told me he'd never considered giving her counselling (he treated her with ECT – shock treatment, as it was called then) because he considered some experiences too painful to be revisited. So he must have known something of her past. But if my father knew, he never spoke of it. The only thing he said that was even remotely connected was, 'When you grow up, Nookie, and have children of your own, you will be grateful you don't have Alley blood in your veins.'

I finally confronted the truth of my mother's childhood in my fiction, in a novel – *River Lines* – written after her death. I don't believe in reincarnation but I have often wished my mother could be born again into a different family, one that would not wreck her chances of happiness at the tender age of seven. Her father's remarriage to the woman who had been helping in the house hardly made things better. With babies arriving on an almost yearly basis, Alice became not so much a half-sister as an unpaid nursemaid, till, at the age of fourteen, she was taken out of school (where she'd been top of her class) for good. From that day on she dreamed of escape, something she finally managed to do at the age of twenty-eight. What followed – putting herself through nursing school, rising to the top of her profession – makes her, in my estimation, a heroine. I'm sure she loved my father when she married him, but I'm equally sure that the marriage, though not the cause of her subsequent descent into madness was, by its very nature a trigger. My father, in her view, was a 'saint'. She was not, nor ever wanted to be.

*****

But I have other, happier memories of 234, ones not connected, or at least not directly, with illness and death. By what I thought at the time must be divine intervention, Uncle Jim and Auntie Grace were living next door to us, at the house we always referred to by its number, 226. Was their decision to move from Gladsmuir at the same time we moved from Lauriston a plan cooked up by the two inseparable brothers? I can't help but believe it was. What did Aunt Bessie, stranded in Braeside, make of this double desertion? Once we got to 234 there were no more card evenings. My mother's erratic health (and behaviour) no doubt put paid to that. But no one stopped me slipping through the creaky gate to reach the haven of my aunt's kitchen, and the comfort of being with someone who was as out of favour with my mother as I was. (The discovery that there were others, all of them women, whom my mother deemed scarcely fit to live was a great comfort to me. I have no idea what Auntie Grace's crime was supposed to have been, but the day she fell from favour we became, and remained, staunch allies.)

Then there were the moments when being eleven or twelve or thirteen created its own universe, one peopled by my friends and my brother's friends, not by those elusive creatures called adults, whose world we would soon be a part of. There were Bible Class camps where Bible study would be followed by dancing and an exchange of chaste, and not so chaste, kisses at the back of the dance hall. There were parties in other people's houses, where the kind of music not allowed in our house was played, and more kisses were exchanged. There was even, on one miraculous occasion, a barn dance in our very own stable. My brother, who could get my mother to agree to just about anything, organised the whole thing, right down to the selection of records and – breaking every rule in the book – a crate of beer. I wore a dress of pale yellow cotton which flared out as I danced. Underneath the skirt was a petticoat made of several layers of tulle. The effect of all that swirling material was magical. One more twirl and I would be airborne. But the dance didn't deliver what it promised. My brother's friends danced with me, but not the boy I fancied myself in love with at the time. He only had eyes for Jennie.

*****

And so a pattern was established: islands of reprieve, when life could feel, for days at a time, almost normal (though the stories my mother told me during these times were anything but); followed, inevitably, by a car or ambulance ride to Ashburn Hall, and long months of absence when either a housekeeper was installed, or we muddled along with help from family and friends. I became expert at making 2/4/6/8 biscuits – 2 eggs, 4 ounces of butter, 6 ounces of sugar, 8 ounces of flour, plus the sultanas my father seemed to crave – but my repertoire in the kitchen was sadly limited. I could manage a roast on Sundays, and corned beef during the week. I could make jellies and junket and rice puddings, and, of course, the inevitable porridge with which the three of us started our days. But that was it.

After the months in Ashburn Hall my mother would return, often not knowing who I was. A burst of frenetic activity would follow: mornings when I would be woken at five to clean the house; afternoons when the ladies from CORSO or the YWCA would be invited for tea, then set to work making clothes for the orphans rescued by Uncle Rewi, my mother's first cousin, who lived (to the dismay of some of my mother's guests) in China; visits from the seemingly endless supply of Somerville and Alley relatives, when I would be ordered to play the piano, even though, to my chagrin, hardly anyone listened.

But more than anything else it was the times when I was the focus of my mother's disgust that I associate with 234. That and my father's death. I wasn't strapped any more. Physical punishment seemed to have been left behind at Lauriston (though it would appear again, with dramatic consequences, when I was in my mid-teens). What my mother began to demonstrate, soon after the move from Lauriston, was something that felt far more threatening. Physical punishment was, after all, a fact of life, both at school and in many other homes I knew, so though I didn't like being hit around the leg with a strap, I didn't feel unduly singled out.

Since I was never given a name for my mother's condition ('nervous breakdown' is the only term I remember hearing), and have only what I can recall of the conversations with Dr Medlicott to go on, I'm forced to speculate about what triggered the change in her soon after we moved to 234. She would have been in her late fifties, well past the menopause, but when I think back on that time when I first became aware of the terrifying fragility of life, I'm convinced the trigger was sex. Before she had treated me with coldness bordering at times on active dislike, but there had also been those periods of remission. Now, though the basic pattern stayed the same, there was a new element – sexual disgust. The only explanation I can come up with, since she was not menopausal, is that it was the onset of *my* periods that triggered this alarming new twist to her mental illness. When I read about T.S. Eliot's wife, Vivian, confined like my mother to a mental hospital, I was struck by the similarities in the two cases. So perhaps, in addition to manic depression, my mother also suffered from a hormone imbalance. (My cousin Pat Alley, a renowned surgeon who boarded with her as a medical student shortly after I left to live with the first of my foster families, believes she suffered from obsessive compulsive disorder or OCD, a condition with no name at the time. Certainly her obsessive cleanliness and need for order fits that pattern, but it was the depression and the mania and, for me, the sexual nature of her taunts, that dominated life at 234.)

I can't pinpoint the exact date when my mother first accused me of sexual misconduct, but it would have been soon after I started at Columba College, the private girls' secondary school my father had insisted I go to (I'd wanted to go to Otago Girls' High School with Jennie). Usually, when I got home from school, I went straight to the sitting room to greet my father (almost completely retired by now). But on this particular day my mother waylaid me.

'Come with me,' she commanded.

Even if I'd wanted to I couldn't have resisted. Her hand was in the small of my back, pushing me out the door I had just walked through.

As we walked down the path that led through the vegetable garden I could smell burning. It was autumn. Mac, the gardener who had replaced Robbie when we moved to 234 (Robbie had grown too old to work) must, I thought, be burning leaves. But when we reached the incinerator there was no sign of Mac, and it wasn't leaves burning in that rusty iron drum, it was my underpants.

'Filthy!' my mother said, spitting out the word, poking at the smoky remains with a stick. 'Disgusting. You are a Jezebel.'

She pulled the glowing stick, trailing streamers of singed cotton, out of the embers, and pointed it at my face. 'Jezebel,' she hissed again.

I don't remember how I got away from her, or where I went. Perhaps I hid in the stables. I never told anyone. I knew that the pants my mother was burning were stained with blood. That made it my fault. I should never have started having periods (soon after this incident they would stop altogether, starting again after a year but from then on 'consistently' irregular). 'Terrible things happen to girls who have anything to do with sailors,' she'd said to me not long after I started primary school. I remembered the words because of where we were at the time. A British warship had berthed at the Dunedin wharf and the four of us had gone to see it. My father and brother had got out of the car to get a closer look but my mother held me back, insisting that a wharf was no place for girls. 'If I ever catch you loitering in this part of town I'll give you a hiding you'll never forget,' she said. At the time I couldn't think what I'd done to make her so angry. But I began to understand that day in the garden.

Over the next few months, till the depression hit again, 'Jezebel' was the name most often on my mother's lips. She would shout it out if she caught sight of me in the street, or if she happened to board the same bus as me. (Did she lie in wait for the bus that would bring me home from my school in the city, or were those humiliating occasions unhappy coincidences? I'll never know.) Down the aisle she would stride, waving her gloved finger, making sure everyone on the bus knew exactly who she was singling out. 'There she is, the brazen hussy! Look at her! Jezebel!'

If the bus driver couldn't persuade her to sit down and be quiet, someone else usually would. It amazed me that people could be so fearless. My friend Fay, daughter of the family across the road, whose home would soon become my sanctuary, had no fear of my mother at all. 'You mustn't talk to Elspeth like that, Mrs Somerville,' she would protest. And before my astonished eyes my mother would get off the bus, meek as a lamb.

*****

Many years later, when, on a brief visit from England, I paid a courtesy visit to Miss Buchan, the retired headmistress of Columba College, another jaw-dropping chapter in the Jezebel saga was revealed to me. Miss Buchan, whom we all feared and mocked behind her back, told me my mother used to ring her up on a regular basis to report that I was sleeping with sailors. 'I would listen politely, thank her for calling, and hang up,' she said, looking at me with an expression I'd never seen on her face before, almost as if we were sharing a joke. I have no idea what I said in response. I suspect I was too stunned to say anything at all. The word I would have chosen to describe the Miss Buchan of my school days was *puritanical*. Any contact with the opposite sex was frowned on. The annual school dance, to take but one instance, was held under the brightest lighting, and policed from the sidelines by our stern headmistress. Yet this same woman had not only protected me from my mother's alarming accusations, she made me her head prefect. Clearly I, like the rest of my classmates, had misjudged her.

As I left Miss Buchan's house on that crisp Dunedin morning, the question knocking about in my head was, how many more people had protected me, and from what exactly?

*****

When I think of this time, when my mother's madness was becoming daily more visible, I have difficulty fitting my brother into the picture. Until my father died he was still at home, still going to King's High School. After my father's death he was sent to board at Waitaki Boys in Oamaru. (I can't imagine my mother agreeing to send the child she loved so far away, so who made that decision? Could it have been Uncle Jim?) What I think was happening, before our world collapsed, was that John was keeping his distance, hanging out with his mates, carving out as good a daily existence as he could from the wreckage of our family life. He was a keen sea scout, passionate about sailing, and he had a boy's typical interest in cars. I imagine these things provided the glue that held him together. I imagine, but I don't know. Already we were going our separate ways.

Chapter Twenty-one

'Wasn't that the definition of home?
Not where you were from, but where you were wanted.'
ABRAHAM VERGHESE, *CUTTING FOR STONE*

After my father died my mother sold 234. I can't pinpoint the date. The years after my father's death are a blur. The islands of reprieve became more and more scattered, till the day my mother lunged at me with a knife, and I escaped by jumping out the window and running across the road to the safety of my friend Fay's home. In a tidy narrative that would be the moment when I left home for good, but life isn't tidy, and though 'Uncle' Charles and 'Aunt' Betty, and their two daughters Fay and Ann, welcomed me into their lives, as if a child fleeing from a murderous mother was as normal as Marmite, for the next few years, until my marriage in 1960, aged twenty, I yo-yoed back and forth from my various foster homes to 234, believing each time there was a reprieve, and my mother wanted me back, that things would change.

Somewhere in that muddied stretch of time my mother had James Anderson's colonial cottage knocked down, and a bungalow without style or character built on the land. I have no memory of that happening, or of the move from 234. Almost everything around that time is a blank. My mother, in the wake of my father's death, had plunged into a panic that only Uncle Jim seemed able to calm. He would patiently rebut her conviction that there was no money and we would all end up in the 'poorhouse', quietly relieving her of the bills that had triggered the panic, talking to her about probate, and assuring her over and over again that Tom had thought of everything when it came to the care of his wife and children.

Then, a year almost to the day after my father's death, Uncle Jim died. Ten years younger than my father, it seemed he (like my mother) could not live without him. Now there was no one to take care of us. Within weeks of Uncle Jim's death my mother was back in Ashburn Hall.

*****

I find it hard now to recreate the times I spent with my mother in the bungalow. In a rare moment of trust she let me paint the room she'd selected to be my bedroom. I chose 'sunset pink'. It was awful. The room was so bright I couldn't sleep.

Each time I went back I found it harder and harder to adjust. At first it was the Smith family home I missed, but later, when the proximity of the two houses started to cause problems – my mother was in the habit of lying in wait for me – I moved in with other kind people: the Reilly family in Macandrew Bay; the family of my history professor, Angus Ross and his wife Margot. So far as I know no money was ever paid to these good people. The trust my father had left was in my mother's control. From the day of my father's death until I married, the only money I had came from a scholarship I was awarded in my last year at school, plus what I earned in the holidays. While I was still at school I took a summer job in a milkbar in Wanaka. That was followed by work on an orchard near Clyde. Then, for two summers in a row, I was employed as cook and nanny on a Canterbury sheep station. When that job disappeared I answered an ad to pick raspberries in Nelson. Unfortunately it rained for most of the six weeks I was there and the crop was ruined, leaving me worse off than before. Unable to go back to my mother's – she was in a manic phase – I took a job as housemistress at my old school, a position I hated, and would eventually be rescued from by Margot Ross.

All this time I believed I was supporting myself, not asking anyone for money, when in fact for most of the time it was the Smiths and the Reillys and the Rosses who fed and housed me.

The home of the first of those families – my near neighbours the Smiths – I regard still as one of the most beautiful I have ever been in. I know nothing of its provenance, but assume its origins were early twentieth century. Set in a large, landscaped garden, with spreading English trees to mark the seasons, and pebbled paths leading to leafy bowers, it entirely suited my imagination at the time, fed as it was on a diet of Victorian and Edwardian fiction. The house seemed designed to fit its surroundings: on all but one side, sets of steps led from French doors into secluded corners of the garden, creating a link between the comforts of the interior and the delights of the carefully cultivated exterior. Like 234 it had a glassed-in veranda from where the garden, in all its myriad moods, could be enjoyed. But unlike 234 this veranda was always warm, a place to go to for conversation, or to listen to music.

Walking through the front door I liked to imagine I was walking onto the set of a movie starring Celia Johnson or Michael Redgrave. The large central hall, with its cosy inglenook fireplace (a fire burned there all day in winter), its oriental rugs, elaborately framed pictures and an arrangement of fresh flowers on the sideboard, transported me in an instant to a world closer to Jane Austen's Pemberley than either Lauriston or 234, where every room testified to the virtues of frugality and plain living. Nor was this impression lessened as I moved through the house. Everywhere I looked there were things to delight the eye: an antique dining table with seating for twelve; cabinets full of priceless glassware and china; twin marble fireplaces in the living room, one at each end, where fires blazed merrily throughout the winter; deliciously comfy sofas and chairs; exotic ornaments, the spoils of foreign travel, lurking in nooks and crannies. Aunt Betty was a niece of the artist Charles Goldie, whose commanding portraits of Maori hung on the walls of the dining room. Other, mostly European, paintings and drawings hung in the living room and the various bedrooms. Even the utility rooms – kitchen, bathroom, laundry – were designed to please. The large Aga cooker in the kitchen meant the room was always warm. The spacious bathroom, with its pale yellow tiles and mirror edged in gilt, created the impression, if not the reality, of a room permanently warmed by the sun.

The first thing I would do on walking into the hall was turn into the living room to say hello to Uncle Charles. For many years a semi-invalid (he had a heart condition), he would invariably be reading in his chair by the fire. The moment he saw me he would discard his book, greeting me in the same way he greeted his daughters, eager to know what had been happening since our last *tête à tête*. Then I would move on to the kitchen where Aunt Betty would be preparing the evening meal, almost certainly something I'd never eaten before – devilled kidneys, beef stroganoff, coq au vin. Wine would be served at dinner (I had my first taste of alcohol in this house), and conversation would flow, while I pinched myself to be sure I wasn't dreaming.

Fay and I shared a room. To have a friend to talk to after the lights were out made it feel as if it were Christmas Eve every night. By this time Jennie and her family had moved to Wellington. Had my life been more settled I would have been inconsolable, but there was so much upheaval going on I remember only a dull sadness, an ache that was by this time as much a part of me as my crooked teeth and flyaway hair.

But 234, and the bungalow with the sunset pink bedroom, were still there. Every morning, waiting for the bus to take me to school, I had to pass the gate that led up winding steps to both houses. 234, having been purchased by a developer who paid my mother far less than it was worth, was being divided into flats. The marble fireplaces were thrown out; the carved ceilings lowered; the ventilators that spoke to me in God's name tossed on the rubbish heap. Soon there would be a forest of letterboxes alongside the one with SOMERVILLE printed on it. And 234 would be divided into A, B, C and D.

*****

The times I spent with the Ross and Reilly families were so happy I managed to forget the reality – my life in the bungalow – for days at a time. I spent only one term with the Reillys but what I most remember of that time was laughter. Pat Reilly and I were in the same class at Columba. We became and have remained good friends. Living with her family in their modern, sun-filled house in Macandrew Bay, studying for exams (it was our last term at Columba and I had Scholarship to sit, as well as preparing for my Trinity College music exams), I felt I'd been given a part in a delightful family comedy. Mrs Reilly's care of her family gave the lie to the notion that a woman stuck at home was missing out on life. Half an hour in her company and you knew she loved her life. Meals – wholesome, home-cooked food, with lashings of fruit cake to satisfy any lingering hunger – were punctuated by jokes as she recounted her adventures with the horses (this, like drinking wine with the Smiths, was a revelation – I'd been brought up to believe that betting on horses was up there with rape and murder). Bedtimes brought more delights – cocoa and cake, and the elixir of encouragement for the day ahead. There was no room in Mrs Reilly's universe for failure. Pat and I were going to sail through our exams, have a triumphant time at university, and live happily every after.

Different delights awaited me on the two occasions I stayed with the Ross family, though there too, despite the geographical distance (the Rosses lived on the other side of town) my mother's shadow followed me. By this time I was at university, studying English, French and History, waiting for the kind of intellectual and emotional excitement I had read about in books to take hold of me. No such thing happened. I worked hard, acted in plays, formed lasting friendships, met the man I would marry, but nothing eclipsed the power my mother continued to exercise over me. My absences from the bungalow had become more frequent and of longer duration – a sign that her depression was waning and a new person was emerging, one who would never confide in me again. I imagine my mother's friends – minus the ones I thought of as secret fairy godmothers – clustering around her, listening to her complaints about my absence, sympathising with her outrage that she was being exposed, by my treachery, as an inadequate mother. To make matters worse Uncle Charles, while I was still living across the road, had made tentative enquiries about adopting me. No doubt my mother got to hear of this and decided enough was enough. I was still a minor. She was my legal guardian. She would use her power to bring me to heel.

The axe fell at the end of my second year at university, while I was living with the Rosses. At my mother's instigation a court order was issued requiring me to live in a hostel. I was devastated. Months had passed since my last summons to the bungalow. Not only had I begun to accept that my relationship with my mother was never going to change, I'd persuaded myself my sojourn with the Rosses would go on until I graduated. The time I spent in their beautiful old house in Alison Crescent I look back on now as among the happiest periods of my life. Angus and Margot had both lost spouses in the war. Margot's husband had died in Egypt, leaving her with a baby daughter – my lifelong friend Jocelyn – to raise on her own. Angus's wife had died while he was serving overseas, leaving him sole parent to a small son. Their marriage, born out of loss and sorrow, was one of the happiest I have known. Margot, whose mind was every bit as sharp as her husband's, worked tirelessly to bring love and security to her reconstituted family. Being, for an enchanted few months, a part of that invigorating household was a gift I treasure to this day.

So my last year at university was spent in a hostel. Most of the students were first-years; I was a third-year but subject to the same restrictive rules. Early in the year I met Fraser Harbutt, a final-year law student. By August we were engaged. By December we were married.

*****

I have come back to live in the bungalow. My mother is lying on her bed. Her lank, unbrushed hair is hanging like wet wool over her shoulders. She who is always so neat and clean, who pulled my mousy hair into a rubber band every morning, as if she thought it would fly away and commit a crime if she didn't restrain it, is wearing pyjamas with a stain on the jacket, lying in a bed that should have smelt of Rinso washing powder and fresh air but smells instead of sickness. She looks at me imploringly.

'Don't let them take me,' she whispers. '*Please*. Don't let them take me.'

I know what she's asking. She's asking me not to send her back to Ashburn Hall, where she will be given shock treatment. My mother, who endures physical pain without a murmur, is terrified of the electricity that will be zapped into her brain. Dr Medlicott has assured me patients being treated with electroconvulsive therapy feel no pain. So why did my mother, last time I accompanied her to hospital, try to jump out of the taxi? I had to pacify not just her but the astonished taxi driver, who was threatening to throw us both out on the side of the road.

I'm not sure what year this is. I've come from the Smiths', so it's either 1958, my first year at university, or early 1959, before I had to move away from Andersons Bay. I don't remember my mother phoning to ask me to come home but that must be what happened. She's ill again – depressed – and when she's in that part of the cycle I'm the person she turns to. It's possible one of my Alley uncles contacted me. Uncle Ron, who lived in Rotorua, would turn up from time to time to try and make sense of my mother's chaotic finances. (She'd already given away almost everything of value from 234. Most of it went to various Somerville cousins, but some went to a missionary she'd taken a shine to.) I doubt it would have been a Somerville relative who made the call. The only one who seemed to grasp the extent of my mother's illness was Tom (like his brother Jack, a Presbyterian minister), but he was far away in Auckland. The rest of the family preferred to think of my mother as 'eccentric', like so many of the Alleys. 'Dear Aunt Alice,' I can hear one cousin in particular saying, 'she does have her funny little ways. All that peering under beds to make sure there's no dust. And the way she scrubs the kitchen floor, it's a wonder there's any linoleum left.'

I tell my mother everything is going to be all right, and go through to the kitchen to make her a cup of tea. How long has she been like this? The house is clean so perhaps only for a day or two. Should I phone the doctor?

I'm still trying to decide what to do when she appears in the doorway and asks me to run a bath for her. I do as she wants, but when I go to leave the bathroom she asks me to stay and shave her armpits for her. I hesitate. My mother and sharp implements is not a good combination. But there is no anger in her today, just a whimpering, murmuring sadness that makes my eyes water, and my breath come in short, painful bursts.

Later, when she's in bed, she starts to talk. This time she tells me about a man she nursed called Paddy de Ranzi. Did I think then that she must have been in love with him? Listening to my mother was always such a nerve-wracking experience, the shock of what she was telling me mingling with the fear I always felt when I was alone with her, that I could never be sure I absorbed what she was really saying. But I remember the way her voice changed as she talked about Paddy, and the expression on her face as she looked at his photo, lovingly preserved in her album.

Paddy de Ranzi was a soldier in the First World War. He was badly gassed in 1917, shipped back home, and would eventually die in hospital. For four years my mother nursed him devotedly. Fascinated, I stare at his photo. A gauntly handsome man in a wheelchair, legs covered by a tartan rug, long, elegant fingers lying limply in his lap, smiles back at me. Unlike other photos in her album this one has withstood the sepia effects of time. Am I imagining it, or do I see a secret in that smile of his, one involving my young mother (she would have been in her late twenties), standing behind him in her crisp white uniform, her hands, guiding the chair, brushing his shoulders.

I listen to my mother talking about him in this strange new voice and I wonder if she ever talked this way about my father. At the time of their marriage she was thirty-nine, my father fifty-nine. I have stared so many times at their wedding photo, trying to decipher its secrets, that I can feel the weight of the fur stole around my mother's neck, and the pinch of my father's starched collar where it presses into his adam's apple. My mother's short dark hair has been tightly waved. She looks as if she's trying to smile. My father's bald head is slightly bowed but he looks happy. He is marrying a woman who knows about human weakness, his own in particular.

I can only imagine the events that preceded that ceremony in the Timaru Nurses' Chapel (where I would be baptised ten years later). It was a warm January day (hardly the weather for fur). The officiating parson was my mother's cousin, Roy Alley. There were only two guests, the nameless witnesses. Am I right in thinking there was something furtive about this wedding? I sense disapproval not just from Aunt Bessie but from the whole Somerville clan. Or is the disapproval emanating from the Alleys? All I know is that my father courted my mother for several years before she agreed to marry him. But when, in the wake of a discovery I made in my forties (of which more later), I asked my cousin Jack if he thought my parents may have had a celibate marriage, I was told I was being ridiculous.

But the facts remain. My father was a bachelor for nearly sixty years. The only female name I'd ever heard mentioned in any sort of romantic connection with him was Minnie Jeffrey, a family friend. According to Aunt Bessie my father broke Minnie's heart. But 'Auntie' Minnie, when I asked her about it, pooh-poohed the idea. 'Goodness me, no. I love your father, everyone does. But marry him? Whatever put that idea into your head?' According to Jack, the explanation for my father's long bachelorhood was to be found in the fairytale notion that he was 'waiting for the right woman'. (Jack himself waited till he was over forty to marry, but he produced three sons and was demonstrably in love with his beautiful wife, Janet.) So what am I to make of the beds on opposite sides of the room, and my mother's aversion to being touched? When I look at the photo of Paddy de Ranzi, and hear again my mother's voice, and watch the changing expression on her face as she tells me his story, I cannot escape the feeling that she had wanted more out of marriage than my father was able to give her.

'Your father is a saint.' Those words, the first time I heard them, in the kitchen at Lauriston, made no sense. Presbyterians don't go in for saints. Neither do Methodists, the religion of the Alleys. Saints belong to the Catholics, sworn enemies, so I'd been taught, of all good Protestants. So what did my father have to do with bodies pierced with arrows, and a woman with her breast cut off? I had to wait till we were living at 234 to have an answer of sorts. Once again enlightenment took place in the kitchen. 'Your father lives in a different world from other men,' my mother announced. 'A higher world.' I've no idea what prompted this declaration, though I imagine Jezebel may have had something to do with it. 'He has nothing to do with the messy business of sex.'

Today, no doubt, someone hearing those words would attach a label, a habit I deplore, since in my experience labels obscure rather than reveal the essential nature of a person. So what if my father was a man who sprinkled lavender water in his bath, rubbed his cheeks with scent after shaving, and allowed his daughter to rub raw onion into his scalp because she'd read somewhere it would restore hair growth? Do these things make him any less of a man? No doubt his habit of walking into milkbars and shouting all the children ice creams would be seen today as a sign of deviation, but in my eyes it was an inextricable part of what made him so loveable (and, it has to be said, recalling how I felt witnessing his more flamboyant public gestures, embarrassing).

You were wrong about my father, I want to say to my mother. He was not a saint. Nor was he Paddy de Ranzi. The fact that he had 'nothing to do with the messy business of sex' doesn't make him saintly, it was just who he was.

*****

Two weeks have passed since my return to the bungalow. My mother is cowering under the bedclothes while Dr Medlicott, summoned after a blur of days, tries, and fails, to get her to talk. 'I'm afraid she'll have to be admitted again,' he tells me after we've gone through to the poky sitting room. 'Can you pack a bag for her?'

Later, travelling with her in the taxi, I feel like a guard accompanying a prisoner to the gallows. She clings to me right up to the moment when the nurse takes her from me and escorts her to her room.

I stagger out into the sunlight. The garden is ablaze with spring flowers. Patients are sitting around on wooden benches talking or reading. It could be a scene out of Jane Austen: Pemberley again, with Elizabeth's extended family in residence. All is serene, settled, *comme il faut*. But as I climb into the waiting taxi my mother's voice beats a drum inside my head. 'Don't let them take me. *Please …*'

*****

Those intermittent returns to the bungalow were the last times I lived with my mother. When I became engaged, at the age of nineteen, I had to secure her permission for the marriage to take place. This could have been an obstacle but my fiancé was the son of a well-known gynaecologist (like many nurses, my mother held doctors, though presumably not psychiatrists, in high esteem) so only a little persuasion was needed to get her to agree to sign the necessary document.

The day of the wedding my mother appeared at the church – the ugly red-brick church of my childhood – dressed entirely in black, with a red gash across her mouth where she had applied lipstick. Dr Medlicott had given her an injection to ensure she stayed calm. He knew about Jezebel. Throughout both ceremony and reception (hosted by Uncle Charles and Aunt Betty) my mother preserved an icy calm. I would not see her again for five and a half years.

Wanaka

'After a certain age, a life exists not for what it really was,
but for its mythological qualities.'
JUSTIN CARTWRIGHT

Chapter Twenty-two

'Memory is an emotional climate,
a thick set of sights and smells and sounds ...'
LISA APPIGNANESI

When I think now of our holiday home, or 'crib' as we called it, in Wanaka, where we went every summer and occasionally in winter, I don't see it, as I did with Lauriston, as larger than it really is, I see it as almost invisible. A corrugated iron lean-to, perched precariously in the shade of a giant pine tree, without electricity or running water, its carbon footprint would have been nil. How the four of us, used to the large draughty rooms of Lauriston and 234, managed in that confined space is a mystery, but my sense is that we were happier there, more of a unit, than we were at home. It no doubt helped that we lived outdoors. Wanaka's summers were almost as reliable as the school bell. On the occasional dull day my mother would produce Chinese chequers and draughts, but the moment the sun came out again my brother and I would be off.

The crib smelt of pine needles and milk. Every morning my father and I would clamber into the Plymouth, parked on the grass next to the crib, and drive around the lake to a farm on the slopes of Mount Roy, where we would get our billies filled with milk for the day. As soon as we got back my mother would decant the milk into jugs, which she would cover with little mesh doilies with tiny beads around the edges. The jugs would then be placed in the safe that sat, like a frozen animal, in the branches of the pine tree. Flies would buzz around, attracted (as I was repelled) by the buttery smells emanating from behind the wire door. To this day I can't stand the smell of milk, or drink it, except heavily disguised in hot drinks.

I have often wondered how my mother, with her nurse's sense of hygiene, coped with those fly-blown, milk-smelling, cicada-singing summers, when meals were cooked on a paraffin stove, and water to wash dishes heated in a thermette.

Did she mind the stink of the dunny, hidden behind a rickety fence at the back of the paddock? I did, although it was the infestation of spiders I minded most. Perhaps what made the holiday bearable for her was the fact that there were no cousins turning up to be fed, just my brother and me, hungry from days spent by the lake or swimming in the town's ugly concrete swimming pool. Or perhaps it was the fact that for those few golden weeks the burden of keeping us safe fell as much on my father's shoulders as on hers. It was he who accompanied us to the lake or the pool, embarrassing us by continuing to wear his business suit, his only concession to the heat being rolled-up shirt sleeves and the knotted hanky perched on top of his head. No other dad looked like him. 'Just as well we're good swimmers,' my brother mutters as we plunge into the chilly water. 'Look at him. He couldn't rescue a mozzie from drowning.'

What did my mother do while we were getting sunburned, or, as happened during two consecutive summers, covered in duck rash? I suspect she lay down on her narrow bed behind the curtain that divided her room from ours, and read. Later, after my father died, she would devour books as if her life depended on them. It should have created a bond between us, since books were where I went to hide too, but for some reason we never talked about what we read. One or other of us would go to the library two, three times a week, but whatever went on in our minds as a result of all this reading, stayed there.

The crib has long gone, diminished even in memory to the point where I begin to wonder if it existed at all. But Wanaka has grown out of all proportion to the dusty, friendly, down-at-heel place I remember. What was a township is now a fully fledged, internationally celebrated tourist centre, site of the kind of house (multiplied many times over) that could hardly have been imagined in the late forties and fifties. I doubt that anyone there these days owns a 'crib'. At some point we stopped owning one too, and began staying at the Wanaka Lodge, a nearby boarding house. Who owned what in the Somerville clan was never clear, so perhaps my father had only part-owned the crib and the land it stood on. There was another family crib at Broad Bay on the Otago Peninsula, but we only ever went there for picnics. Wanaka, on the other hand, felt like ours. Even when we'd given up 'baching' and moved to the Lodge, the sense of ownership clung to us like the smell of pine trees and the persistent tickle of heat on our bodies.

It was at Wanaka that I finally grasped the fact that my father was an old man. He used to take himself off every morning for what my mother called his 'constitutional'. Curious as to what this was, and reluctant as always to let him out of my sight, I followed him one day. Clutching a towel and an old cushion, he headed for the path that led through stunted bush and clumps of yellow gorse to a small grassy plateau halfway up the hill behind the Lodge. The day was blisteringly hot, the air pungent with the dusty smells of summer. When my father (who walked with the aid of a stick) reached his destination, I quickly buried myself in the warm tussock and waited to see what he would do. To my shocked astonishment, he began to undress. A man who seemed never to take his suit off was slowly revealing himself as a man who wore strange underpants and a large elastic bandage around his middle. His legs, once the long-johns had been removed, looked like pale sticks, decorated with brown spots and thistledown hair and squiggles of blue embroidery sewn by a five-year-old. His arms were the same. For so long I'd thought of him as plump – I still own a tiny brass Buddha, souvenir of his travelling days, which as a four-year-old I christened 'my little fat daddy' – but my father wasn't plump at all: he was barely there.

I stared in horror at the apparition in front of me. Bandages meant wounds. Was my father bleeding under that bandage? Was he going to die? Unable to stop watching I waited as, with the bandage still intact, he slowly lowered himself onto the towel at his feet, sitting for a moment before sinking, with a loud sigh, onto the ground.

I've no idea how long I crouched there, aching with love and sunburn. I only know that after that day things were different. The evidence had been there all the time: the baldness, the deafness, the teeth taken out at night and deposited in a glass of disinfectant, the walking stick. I just hadn't wanted to see it. Before that day I'd been known as a chatterbox. My mother was always reprimanding me for 'showing off'. Apparently I could 'talk the hind leg off a donkey'. But for a long time after that revelation on the hillside I didn't talk much at all. What I did was watch my father. The slightest sign of tiredness and I would rush to his side, questions flying out of my mouth like orange pips: 'What's the matter?' 'Are you all right?' 'Shall I make a cup of tea?' 'Would you like to play cards?' 'Shall I fetch your slippers?' And if anyone in the school playground dared to suggest my father was not my father but my grandfather, I would use my fists.

*****

'And the moon shines bright on Janet Porter/ For she's a snorter/ And so's her daughter/ And they wash their feet in soapy water/ And so they oughta/ To keep them clean …' This was my father's Wanaka song, sung or hummed in place of 'My Wife She Died and I Laughed and I Cried'. I accepted the change, as I accepted everything about him, without question, but on our last ever family holiday I discovered why he chose to sing this song and not his usual anthem. I was twelve years old and experiencing the first pangs of love. The object of my interest was a plump boy called David, who was staying at the Lodge with his parents. Holding hands with David was such a momentous experience I lost interest for a time in anything else. It was David who enlightened me as to what was going on. The owner of the Lodge, a woman with bright yellow hair and a croaky laugh, was called Janet Porter. How come I'd not noticed that before? It all made sense. My father was an inveterate tease (though I never heard him tease my mother). Every time 'Mrs Porter' came into the room he would start humming her tune. She must have been a 'good sport', which, as everyone knew, is what the person being teased is expected to be (a test I often failed when my brother was doing the teasing), because she invariably laughed. My father would grin at her, and for a few golden moments I would forget about the bandage, and the stick-thin legs, and the sighs no one was meant to hear, and believe again in my mother's immortal elixirs.

Was this the summer when my mother told me she would be going into hospital? No, that must have been earlier, just before my tenth birthday. We were walking back from the township, carrying the day's provisions. I remember being surprised when my mother suggested I go shopping with her. Normally she went with my father in the car, leaving my brother and me to wander at will, the only rule being that we didn't go near the lake. This day was different.

My mother is wearing a green seersucker sunfrock with a matching bolero. Her hair, which is usually tied back in a roll and secured with a hairnet, is hanging loose. She is suddenly beautiful, and young (she is fifty-seven). I am too awestruck to do more than trot alongside her, trying not to scuff my feet through the gravel (that would annoy her), trying not to be a chatterbox. She doesn't say much. At one point she asks me about school, and I start to tell her about Jennie and our hut in the macrocarpa hedge, but she stops me with an irritable wave of her hand.

We reach the township, and head for the General Store. My mother takes out her list, and I watch as her basket fills with packets of jelly and processed cheese, two loaves of bread, a lettuce with dirt sticking to its roots, a brown paper bag full of tomatoes. While she chats to the storekeeper I'm allowed to wander deep into his Aladdin's Cave. Jackets, trousers, shirts, frocks hang down from the ceiling, batting my face as I push through the thickets to reach the back, where bins of flour and sugar stand alongside drawers marked 'Underpants', 'Singlets', 'Socks', 'Wool'. A box of Christmas cards sits forlornly on top of one of the chests. Another box marked 'Nails' sits next to it. There are coils of rope, and shaky pyramids of buckets and saucepans, and one whole corner stacked with garden tools and gumboots. Perhaps if I look hard enough I'll find Aladdin's lamp, and the genie who will lead me to the hidden treasure.

'Come along, Elspeth!' My mother's voice brings me scuttling back into the sunlight. She hands me a paper bag filled with apricots, cautions me against squashing them, and we set off down the hill, past the picture house where, on special Saturday afternoons, my brother and I are allowed to go and see *Bambi* or *Hop-along Cassidy* or *Snow White and the Seven Dwarfs*.

I glance at my mother but her face tells me nothing. It's as if someone has turned a lock, and her eyes, nose and mouth are in prison, unable to move. I've seen this look before. It frightens me.

We reach the road that leads to the Lodge, and start to walk beside the lake. I fix my eyes on the faintly rippling water, anticipating the moment when my brother and I will run, laughing and splashing each other, into those tiny, blissfully cooling waves. A handful of boats bob about on the water but they barely interrupt the view. I can see straight across to Mount Roy and Glendhu Bay. And I can see, ahead of us, Ruby Island, with its spires of pine trees and its forbidden stories. (Another conversation I wasn't meant to hear: Ruby Island, host to wild dance parties in the 1920s, site of a long ago Maori battle. My ignorance of all things Maori is something I will only become aware of, and ashamed of, years later. For now they are too 'other' to enter my imagination. They belong with other things I have read about but can't relate to – the Jabberwocky and the Tumtum Tree.)

'I have to tell you something,' my mother says. We've been walking for more than ten minutes. 'I want you to listen very carefully.'

I glance at her, but her head is turned away so I can't see the expression on her face. It's as if she's saying these things to a mirror. Mirror mirror on the wall …

'I don't want you to worry,' she says. 'People will help. All sorts of people. You can be sure of that.' She sniffs, wriggling her nose as if to let it out of its prison. 'I'm not well. That's what I have to tell you. I'll be going into hospital when we get back home. Aunt Bessie has offered to look after you but I don't want that. It would mean her and Uncle Harry coming to live at Lauriston, and I don't think you'd like that much, would you?' She doesn't wait for me to answer. She doesn't even look at me. 'I want you to look after your father and brother. Do you think you can do that?'

This time she does look at me. I bite my lip, and try to think of the right answer, but nothing comes. 'I've taught you how to cook and make beds, and you know how to light the copper for the washing. Tom' – she quickly corrects herself – 'your father will find someone to come and help, so you won't have to do everything. But I want you to see that things are done properly, especially where your father is concerned. It's important his routine isn't interrupted.'

The words swirl around in my head like the chips of glass in a kaleidoscope. I have no idea what pattern they will make when they finally stop moving. My mother is ill. She's going to hospital. I'm to take her place. I'm the one she trusts. Does that mean she loves me after all? But how can I do all the things she wants me to do and still go to school? She must be really sick if she's going to hospital. Is she going to die?

'Well?' she says.

I nod furiously. I'm trying not to cry. I don't want my mother to die. But I don't want her to call me a cry baby either, so I fight back the tears and keep nodding.

'Cat got your tongue? That makes a change.'

'I don't want you to be sick,' I mutter.

She gives me the faintest of smiles. 'I'm afraid I don't have much choice in the matter,' she answers.

'I'll do everything you say. I *promise.*'

'Of course you will. I've trained you well. You're my star probationer.'

Probationer … It's what she called me when she taught me how to make a bed with hospital corners, and again when she showed me how to clean the lavatory so no Bertie Germs could escape and make us sick. Sue Barton, in the first book in the series I read to please her, was a probationer nurse. So now I'm to be one, is what she's saying. I feel a tingling down my spine. I won't let her down. I will strain carrots for my father's juice, and make porridge the way he likes it for his breakfast, and remember to heat the pot when I make his tea, and she will be so proud of me. I don't even mind if I miss school.

*****

Three days after our return to Dunedin my mother disappears. I don't see her again for over a month. No one tells me what's wrong with her. I get up at 6 o'clock and make the porridge and the school lunches, and sweep the kitchen floor. Then, if it's a day when no one is coming to help, I gather up the dirty washing and put it in the copper ready for washing day. Finally I take my father's breakfast through to him on a tray, taking care to do everything as my mother instructed. I've put a cup of cream and a bowl of honey beside the porridge, which I've already sprinkled with Bemax, and I've made tea the way he likes it, heating the pot first, then letting it stand for seven minutes. 'And how's my Nookity this morning?' he asks as I push open the door.

'Box of birds,' I answer. 'And how's my Poppity?'

My brother and I walk to school so there's no need for my father to get up (he is semi-retired by this time). Later he will go and visit our mother in hospital, but John and I only get to see her on Sundays, and sometimes, when she is too unwell, not even then.

Sometime in the middle of this period Aunt Bessie tells me about the sulphur drugs. I know she does it to comfort me, but as I don't really understand what she's saying her good intentions fall on stony ground.

The first time we go to the hospital, a month after my mother was admitted, we're only allowed to be with her for a few minutes. We find her sitting up in bed, wearing a pink bedjacket with a satin bow. She smiles at us, but it's the kind of smile that isn't directed at anyone. 'The children are here, Alice,' Dad prompts, pushing John forward to make sure she can see him. She doesn't respond, just goes on smiling. I can feel John pulling at my sleeve, anxious to be gone from this strange-smelling place with its white walls and hushed noises. I want to be gone too. I don't know the lady in the bed. It isn't our mother. She doesn't even look like her.

'Sorry, kiddywinks,' Dad says as he ushers us out of the room. 'Your mother's still not well. May be best if you wait till she's better.'

'What's the matter with her?' John mumbles.

'That's what we're trying to find out,' Dad answers.

Three months later my mother returns home, but things don't go back to the way they were. From now on, till I leave home forever, she will be in and out of hospital, only this time it won't be the one in Stafford Street, where she used to nurse, but Ashburn Hall. We still manage to have holidays in Wanaka, my mother still makes my father's immortal elixir, the family still comes en masse for Christmas, but for much of the time my mother doesn't know who I am. She calls my brother and father by their names, but I either have no name or I'm mistaken for one of her sisters. I'm Aimée or Vera or Clarice. Till I become 'Jezebel', a name that will stick.

MEMORIES OF A CHILDHOOD HOLIDAY

In the sun-drenched past
two children run beside the water's edge

The girl is pot-bellied, straight-haired,
her ears, her mother's told her,
resemble a rabbit's.
The boy is dark, his hair curls,
he's learning what it is to be embarrassed

Their father sits in a willow's shade,
white hanky knotted on his head

'And the moon shines bright on Janet Porter,
for she's a snorter,
and so's her daughter,
and they wash their feet in soapy water,
and so they oughta
to keep them clean'

The real Janet Porter laughs.
Her head is swathed in a rainbow scarf.
'Is she a gypsy?' the girl enquires.
Her father lights his pipe, and smiles

Janet Porter owns the Lodge.
'She lives with a man,' their father says.
'Not Mr and Mrs, friends.'

'Sticks and stones may break my bones
but names will never hurt me'

The boy and girl run beside the water's edge

The town is a ship –
hill plunging into lake
hotel moored to a gravel slope.
Words are a puzzle
Town-ship.
Hotel, synonymous with sin

The boy and girl run beside the water's edge

'Oh I'm itchy, I'm itchy, I'm itchy, I'm itchy,
oh I'm itchy, I'm itchy, I'm itchy, I am'

Brother and sister furiously sing,
slosh cold water on their reddened skin,
compare duck-rash tattoos, bruises,
and the curious differences between them

'I told you not to let them swim,' they hear their
    mother say,
her voice tight as an unwound skein of wool.
'No harm done,' their father reassures,
'not measles after all.'
'What's the matter with the pool?'
'Apparently,' the doctor says,
'white youngsters get it worse.
Something to do with the colour of their skin.'

The boy and girl run beside the water's edge

'Here and here and here
our ancestral people lie.'
Tuhawaiki's words, learned later,
puzzle too.
Measles, the girl reads, killed thousands

Ducks quack dangerously among the rotting weeds,
lake froths against the hotel wall,
rain scars water sky and hill

'Miss Bun, the Baker's daughter?' the boy requests.
'No!' the girl snaps. 'I've got no Buns at all!'

The boy and girl run beside the water's edge

'Mrs M Mrs I Mrs S-S-I
Mrs S-S-I, Mrs P-P-I'

Colourful as a postcard
the steamer chugs towards the wild Matukituk.
A voice intones the lake's height, width, depth

Te Wai Pounamu: Water of Green Talc

'Never let it be said,' the mother whispers,
'that you and your brother are not ours.'

The boy and girl run beside the water's edge

'Compliments of the season,' their father beams,
pushing through the rows of shirts
flapping round his head, like bats.
The General Store is an Aladdin's Cave.
It smells of rope and the colour grey.
'And the same to you,' the answer comes.
'And Mrs S, of course. Keeping well I trust?'

Never let it be said …

'Not so good, I'm afraid,
The old trouble again.'

'Our Father which art in heaven …'

The boy and girl run beside the water's edge

'Aw come on Mum, please' –
shadows on the mother's face,
the boy seems not to see –
'John Wayne, Mum. Don't be mean.'

The girl hangs back to watch –
Seersucker dress, green as new grass,
grey hair captured in a net

'She loves me, she loves me not,
she loves me, she loves me not …'

'We go home soon, Mum. Be a pal.'

The picture house is a Palace,
it's made of wood and tin.
'You're barmy, you're barmy
Your mother's in the army'

Six men wait in a truck from out of town.
'Hey Skinny! That your brother or what?'
On every lip a curling froth of beer.
'Ask him to show you what he's got between his legs!'
'Cock-a doodle-do!'

Mrs M Mrs I …
Our Father which art …
Never let it be said …
This lake is thirty miles …

The boy and girl run beside the water's edge

In the hills, among the gorse and pine
their father strips his clothes off.
The girl, patrolling, spies
the knotted hanky first,
then the chest, flat like her own

Do all men take their clothes off in the sun?

'Again and again and again
Again and again and again, again,
my wife she died
and I laughed and I cried,
for I was single again.'

Days when he hums, days when he whistles,
days when he sings.

And the moon shines bright on Janet Porter …

These hills are full of voices

'Nothing to worry about, my dears,
your mother'll soon be home.'
'What's the matter with her?'
'She's tired, that's all.
When you grow up you'll understand.'

The father kneels beside his bed.
The girl, concealed, watches.
Don't cry, she wills. Oh please don't cry.

'Jesus loves me this I know,
for the Bible tells me so …'

Outside the town
a wooden shed called Church of Saint Ignatius,
its corrugated roof reminds the girl of blood.
'Bloody tykes!' the boy explodes,
'Catch me with one of them!'

Cock-a doodle-do …

Their own church is built of stone

'Are Catholics bad?' the girl enquires.
Their father shakes his head, and frowns.
'Are Germans?'

Behind the car the lake is stretched with light.
A cloud of dust goes with them.
'Young lady,' the father says,
his face a moon of love,
'You ask too many questions.'

*****

After my father's death there are no more holidays in Wanaka. There are no more holidays at all. But though my life has changed, irrevocably, Wanaka is still Wanaka. The seismic changes that will transform it almost beyond recognition are still some way off. So I go back, not for a holiday but to work in the milkbar on the main street. Even when other jobs take the place of that first foray into the world of paid work, I contrive to get back to Wanaka whenever I can. Part of my camping honeymoon is spent there, though by that time I am no longer Elspeth Somerville, I am Susan

Harbutt. My new young sisters-in-law have difficulty pronouncing Elspeth (though they have since denied this), so I become Susan. A married woman, with a bank account, and a home of her own.

PART FOUR: FOOTSTEPS

'Time which eats the stories of our lives
Preserves a cruel freshness here to show
How energetic certainty contrives
To tell us what we think we almost know.'
PETER PORTER

Chapter Twenty-three

'The past was never the past,
it's what made the present able to live with itself.'
JULIAN BARNES

'I don't believe in God, I only believe in Jesus.'

'You can't say that.'

'I just did.'

'God is Jesus's father. They go together.'

'Joseph. He's the father. Joseph and Mary. His mum and dad.'

It's my first theological discussion. John and I are walking across the paddocks behind Lauriston on our way to school. I'm five, John is seven. It's my favourite time of day. I have all those hours in the classroom to look forward to – no 'creeping like snail unwillingly to school' for me – and I have this time, trailing barefoot (our shoes are keeping dry in our school bags) through damp pungent grass, with my adored older brother.

Our journey stretches from one Somerville home, Lauriston, past another, Gladsmuir; to the third, Braemar, where Aunt Bessie, maker of mouth-watering scones and cakes, dispenser of domestic wisdom, lives with the black bat, Uncle Harry. When I'm older, and no longer needing John's protection, I will often call in at Braemar on my way home from school. The cake tins are always full, and the dreaded Uncle Harry – his son has a coal delivery business: for a long time I think this explains why Uncle Harry always wears black – is mercifully absent during the day.

I love Aunt Bessie. Cast out from Lauriston when my father married, obliged some years later to become housekeeper in her own home to her widowed brother-in-law, she could be described as a stereotypical old maid, forced to follow where others led, but she was never that to me. The words that come out of her mouth are too surprising. Ditto her habit, indulged by her brothers, of cheating at cards. A Good Woman who Cheats: my lifelong love of paradox, seeded in Braeside's aromatic kitchen.

Aunt Bessie's appearance never varies. She wears a version of the same smudgy floral frock, day in day out, the only variation being in the basic colour – grey, navy or black. Over this she wears an apron – she calls it a *pinny* – made of sacking and large enough to cover her capacious bosom. She has very little hair on her head (baldness is a Somerville affliction); far more growing on her face and chin. To all intents and purposes a staunch Presbyterian, she can shock with a sudden cutting dismissal of a disappointing sermon or a member of the congregation who has earned her disapproval. Rules, she tells me, in those moments when her guard is down, are there to be broken. 'God gave you two good hands' – this in the middle of a cooking lesson – 'why do you need a wooden spoon?'

But it's the things she lets drop about my mother that explain, more than the scones and cakes and cookery lessons, my enthusiasm for visiting Braemar. 'Alice's trouble is she doesn't know how to sweep the dirt under the carpet.' 'Your mother should have been a man. She doesn't like women. Never has.' 'Your father had his work cut out when you came on the scene, I can tell you. A female child was the last thing your mother wanted.'

'Tell me more,' I urge at these times.

'Why did Tom have to marry at all? I did everything for him. He never wanted for a thing. And why choose that woman, in God's dear name? If he had to have a wife, why couldn't it be Minnie Jeffrey? They were sweethearts for years. Minnie still carries a candle, poor soul. I could have borne it if it had been Minnie ...'

Another glimpse into the mystery of my father. Another 'aunt' to seek out and question.

But I'm getting ahead of myself. John and I are still on our way to school. The theological discussion has been replaced by an ethical one. Is it wrong to steal eggs from a bird's nest? John, ever the intrepid climber, has spotted a nest in the branches of the silver birch tree by the gate that leads into Gladsmuir. To whimpers of protest from me he has shimmied up the trunk, and is now holding high in the air a perfect blue egg with tiny brown specks on it. 'Put it back,' I hiss. 'It's got a baby inside. Put it back.'

But John puts it in his pocket.

We trudge on through the bush, stopping to shoot convolvulus flowers at each other, chanting 'Fly away Peter, fly away Paul'. I have no idea what the words mean but I like the way they sound. Soon we're chanting the whole rhyme. 'Two little dicky birds sitting on a wall, one named Peter, one named Paul. Fly away Peter, fly away Paul. Come back Peter, come back Paul.' But the bell-shaped flowers John and I catapult at each other are non-retrievable. Like the bird inside the egg in my brother's pocket.

We emerge from the bush to the sound of the school bell ringing. We've dawdled too long. We pull on our shoes and socks, leaving the laces undone, and run the last few yards to school. I sprint down the hill to the Primer One classroom; John goes up the hill to Primer Four. We won't see each other again till 3 o'clock when school ends. But at lunchtime we will unpack the same food: Marmite and lettuce sandwiches; a raw carrot; a few raisins; an apple. No drink, because the school provides it in the form of bottled milk, which I loathe. It's bad enough that I have to drink each night, under my mother's watchful eye, a cup of boiled milk with a thick skin on top (there's been a Tb scare: my mother boils milk as a precaution). That I can't escape. School milk is another matter. By the time the bottles are handed out at morning playtime they have been sitting, sometimes in full sunlight, for over an hour. Intended to foster the health of the nation, those free drinks are my daily torment. That is until I come up with a solution: a rota of classmates whom I have persuaded to relieve me of the hated white stuff. Two of them are from the orphanage. I tell myself I'm being kind giving it to them, as they probably don't have enough to eat, but I know, even as I think it, that it's not true. (Soon I will know about the diet at the orphanage from personal experience. My father, chairman of the orphanage committee, hearing that the orphans were being teased at school, sent my brother and me to live with them for a week. Teasing orphans, we were informed, with atypical sternness, was a sin. God loved orphans every bit as much as he loved us. That week turned out to be one of the happiest of my life. Sleeping in a dormitory with other whispering girls, I had neither nightmares nor nose bleeds. As for the regime, with its timetables and its code of discipline, it differed only in details from the one my mother imposed at home.)

Years later, when I'm living as far from New Zealand as it's possible to get, I fall into the habit of describing my mother as a 'food Nazi'. Making jokes about her has become a coping strategy. My mother was a fanatic about food and health long before such passions were fashionable. Sweets were forbidden in our house, as was chocolate. The only sweetener my brother and I were allowed was honey. Describing my mother in this way helps me to live with my memory of her, but the truth is, had I not grown up with a 'food Nazi' I might now be a hunchback with poor teeth and spotty skin.

When my mother discovered I had a double curvature of the spine I was put on a special calcium-enriched diet (she never knew about the palmed-off school milk), and ordered to lie on a wooden board for an hour a day. Twice a week I was taken for treatment at the Physiotherapy School, where I swam in the pool, and was massaged. My mother was determined that her children, the loved and the unloved, would be physically perfect. No one would ever accuse her of neglect. I remember her outrage when the school dental nurse filled what my mother swore was a non-existent hole in my teeth. Watching the hapless nurse tremble in the face of my mother's wrath gave me a thrill of pleasure. Now someone else knew what it was like to be held in thrall to that mouth full of scalding words, and those eyes that drilled holes in your skin.

But when I'm with my brother I don't think about my mother. I'm safe when he's with me, though not as safe as when my father is at home. John, at the age of seven, is a natural rebel, and since I want nothing more than to *be* him, I'm fast becoming a rebel too. Finding someone else to drink my school milk is my first act of rebellion. Swapping my healthy sandwiches for white bread versions, dripping with butter and jam, is my second. The third, the most wicked of all, involves skipping out of school at lunchtime, clutching my week's pocket money, to join the other lucky kids making a dash for the pie shop at the tram terminus. Sinking my teeth into a warm mince pie, juicy with gravy and bursting with flavour, is like diving into a warm sea.

I love school. To me it's a Brave New World where the rules make sense, and adults behave more or less predictably. On my first day at school I was so incensed when the bell rang and everyone started to go home, I rang it again to bring everyone back. (The bell was in the Primer One classroom, out of reach of five-year-olds, but a chair on top of a desk solved that problem.) I don't remember being punished for this outrage but I do remember my brother's shocked disbelief when my trespass was discovered. John spends his time at school waiting for that final bell to ring so he can escape to his hut in the macrocarpa hedge: I spend the last few minutes of each school day with my hands over my ears.

And so the pattern of life till my school days come to an end is created. I have found my place of safety, a refuge far more secure than a hut in the hedge or a stable attic. School is my ticket of leave.

Chapter Twenty-four

'A faithful friend is the medicine of life.'
ECCLESIASTES

Of course not everything about Andersons Bay Primary School was wonderful. I may have felt safer there than I did at home but the regime was strict – corporal punishment was commonplace, and the fear of being caught out in some misdemeanour never far away. Rebellion was exciting, but not the thought of the punishment that would follow if caught. Besides, I was not a natural rebel. My need to be liked, especially by those with authority over me, kept getting in the way.

Until the age of nine school was a balancing act between the rebellion necessary for me to preserve a sense of myself as brave, like my brother, and the behaviour that would earn me the approval of my teachers. But in my Standard Three year something happened that changed the way I saw the world and my own place in it. This event – really a series of events – would lead, thirty years later, to my novel, *Finding Out*. (I'm forced to agree with the statement, made by a discerning critic, that all novels, no matter how distant from the lived life of the author, retain traces of 'biographical mud'.)

But first it is necessary for me to properly introduce my friend Jennie. Little did I know when, at the age of eight, I was assigned the task of looking after the new girl in class, that she would not only become a lifelong friend, but would succeed, where I had failed, in discovering the identity of my birth family. Jennie's family – mother, father, three children – had moved to Dunedin from New Plymouth, a town that meant nothing to me at the time. As far as I was concerned New Plymouth might as well have been another country.

Before long Jennie's home became, like Braemar, a place I was drawn to, like a moth to light. Jennie's mother was beautiful, serene and kind, as different from my own mother as it was possible to be. On the few occasions I was allowed to spend a weekend with the family at their crib in Purakanui, I would become sick with happiness (a paradox that still afflicts me – bring me good news, and chances are I will throw up). Jennie's father, a gentle bear of a man, showered affection on his children and on his wife. This to me was a revelation. I had never seen my parents kiss, or touch other than accidentally. Jennie's parents called each other 'darling', walked with their arms around each other, and, most startling of all, shared a bed. It was a glimpse into another universe.

By the time we had risen to the dizzy heights of Standard Three Jennie and I were inseparable. Our teacher was a young man whom I will call Jimmy Penrose. At first this was exciting. All our teachers till now had been women. For a while, till things began to happen which neither of us had words for, Jennie and I, secure in our hut in the macrocarpa hedge, acted out fantasies about Mr Penrose which a psychiatrist would no doubt have a field day interpreting. Some of this crept into *Finding Out*, but the story I tell there concerns a teacher whose instincts are basically good. What Jimmy Penrose was about did not feel so benign. (At a school reunion in 2008 – the only reunion I have ever attended – Jennie and I were astounded to see, among the hundreds of people listening to the speeches, a stooped old man whose identity age had done little to conceal. Without thinking, I poked my tongue out at him, something I would never have dared do sixty years earlier; a long-delayed act of rebellion.)

Jimmy Penrose liked to use the strap. He was not unusual in that. What *was* unusual was his liking for strapping me. I was not a naughty child. School was my safe haven. No way would I have risked compromising that. But I did have one chronic defect and that was my inability to shut up. I loved telling stories. And I loved hearing them, so I was forever either whispering to the person in the desk next to me, or listening intently to what he or she had to say. If this infuriated Mr Penrose I never saw any sign of it. Every time he asked who was talking, and my hand went up, he would smile, as if giving me four sharp whacks on my open palm was the thing he most wanted to be doing. Afterwards he would sidle up to my desk, stroke my red and swollen hand, and whisper, 'Is it still hurting? Shall I make it better for you?' Often he would linger, playing with the bracelet I wore every day – the one I believed was from my birth mother – saying how beautiful it was, and asking who had given it to me. I never told him.

For a few agonising months I held the record for being strapped more than any other child in the school. Though I never told my parents about it, word must have got out, because from one day to the next Jimmy Penrose was gone. Nothing was said. Now when I try to piece together what might have happened the person I think of is Albert Benson, son of the local butcher. Albert had more than once taken punishment intended for me. It would happen like this: Mr Penrose, busy writing on the blackboard, would suddenly spin around and bark, 'Who's talking?' Even if I didn't put my hand up he would assume it was me, but sometimes Albert, who wasn't talking at all, would put his hand up. The punishment he received was always particularly savage: six cuts to the hand, not four. On one never-to-be forgotten day, as I was walking down the corridor, about to head home across the paddocks, I heard a sound of a cane being wielded, and a low whimpering as the cane met its target. I looked into the classroom – our classroom – and there was Albert stretched across the table, receiving an enthusiastic caning from Mr Penrose. To this day I cannot bear to witness scenes of corporal punishment in movies. Invariably the faces I see are those of Jimmy Penrose and Albert: the former no longer human; the latter enduring this terrible punishment because of me.

I would like to think Albert was braver than I was and told his parents, and I have him to thank for the end of our mutual torment. Whether he did or not, from that day on he and I were firm friends. I supplied him with Santé chocolate bars, bought with my pocket money, and he supplied me with pineapple chunks, a ritual broken only when we reached Standard Five and considered ourselves too old for such childish gestures.

*****

If I don't now remember Standard Three as an *annus miserabilis* it is because of my friendship with Jennie. Her gift of empathy meant I was never alone with what was happening. Even when the time we spent in our hut was taken up not with play-acting but with whispered attempts to understand what was going on, the nature of the bond between us was such that it seemed we were both caught up in these events. Better still was the feeling that if we kept talking about them they would, eventually, make sense.

Two years later something happened that would ensure my friendship with Jennie would last for the rest of my life. We were by this time in Standard Five. Our teacher was Winifred Dent, a woman I admired for reasons I knew would not find favour with my parents. Mrs Dent was a divorcée. In 1951 Dunedin that was tantamount to being a 'scarlet woman'. Had I read Hawthorne's blistering novel *The Scarlet Woman* by then? I don't think so, though I had started on my indiscriminate reading from my father's library, acquiring along the way a precocious if somewhat skewed idea of what went on between the sexes. I knew what divorce was, but when I looked at Mrs Dent I didn't see a woman who had sinned, but someone who had experienced momentous things, way beyond my comprehension but not beyond my imagination.

Mrs Dent was beautiful. Or so I thought at age eleven. She dressed in colourful clothes that would have been as out of place in my mother's wardrobe as the bikinis that were just then coming into fashion. She wore nylon stockings and high-heeled shoes, and dainty pearl earrings. Her lips and nails were bright red; her hair curled prettily around her face, indisputable evidence that she was not plain, like me.

I fell in love with Mrs Dent. I'd stopped wanting to be my brother by this time – he was at secondary school, on another planet – so wanting to be Mrs Dent simply filled the gap my brother had left. Was she aware of my hero-worship? Probably. She would certainly have been aware of my status as an adopted – ie illegitimate – child. Perhaps she saw us both as outcasts, and that explained her turning me into her 'pet', a term of opprobrium that, before long, was following me around like a bad smell.

It took a while for the full impact of this new label to sink in. I was the clever kid in class. The only subject I performed badly in was art. I'd been called a lot of names over the years – 'clever clogs', 'dirty swot', 'stuck up' – but I'd never been a 'teacher's pet' before. Slowly it dawned on me that fewer and fewer people were talking to me. Even Albert Benson and his buddy Ian Macandrew, my closest rival for academic honours, began to slink away. They were encouraged in this by a girl called Beverley, whose dislike of me was something I had tried hard (too hard, probably) to dislodge. There were jibes about my parents not being my real parents; about them being old enough to be my grandparents; about my mother's cousin, Rewi Alley, whose visits to our house from communist China, confirmed my pariah status. There were even jibes about my often spectacular nose bleeds, curse of my first two decades of life.

Finally the day came when no one was talking to me at all, not even Jennie. But this, the lowest moment in my school life, far worse than the punishments meted out by Jimmy Penrose, was merely the dark before the dawn. Jennie, briefly persuaded to join the class decision to send me to Coventry, was made of sterner stuff than Beverley and her cohorts.

I'm standing by the school fence, fingers entwined in the wire, a glimpse of the harbour in the distance. Behind me Beverley has mustered her troops. The boys are playing in their part of the playground, but Beverley has the girls where she wants them. I can hear the thwack thwack of the skipping rope, and the chant that accompanies the game. 'Salute to the Captain, Bow to the Queen, And turn your back on the Nazi submarine ...'

I don't look round. This has been going on for weeks. I've developed a strategy to cope with it, imagining I am someone else, some*where* else. Today I'm a concert pianist, playing to a rapt audience. Sitting where I can see him is my father, his eyes wet with tears as I play the music I tell myself he loves (though really it's my mother who loves music: my father is tone deaf). What does a silly skipping game matter? Who cares about Beverley when you have friends like Schubert and Mozart? That's when I feel it, the tap on my shoulder. I look around: Jennie, her face contorted as if she's waiting for a needle to be stuck in her arm, looks back at me. I peer over her shoulder and see Beverley standing in front of her troops, staring across the wide expanse of playground. Jennie must have crossed that asphalt desert by herself. A walk as long and lonely as Gary Cooper's down the main street of Hadleyville, Kansas.

'Wannaplayhopscotch?' Jennie mumbles.

What did I say in answer? I don't remember. Probably it didn't involve words. But from that day on Beverley's power is at an end, and I have a friend for life.

Chapter Twenty-five

*'During certain hours, at certain years in our lives,
we see ourselves as remnants from the
earlier generations that were destroyed.'*
MICHAEL ONDAATJE, *RUNNING IN THE FAMILY*

I don't know when the concept of the fairy godmother first entered my consciousness but I can see now, looking back, that I had several fairy godmothers, all of them benign. The story of the wicked fairy, which I read in my father's book of *Grimm's Fairy Tales*, made an awful kind of sense to me, struggling to learn how to sew under my mother's tutelage, but it never seriously dented my faith in the good fairies hovering about me as I grew up. Three of these mysterious women (only now do I realise how little I knew about them) were friends of my mother's, but far from finding fault with me, they expressed approval of my efforts, whether it was in the kitchen, cooking during my mother's many absences; or on the tennis court (my birth father played tennis at national level – despite my lack of interest in competitive sports it seems I inherited some of his talent); in the schoolroom; or playing the piano. My academic successes – achieved, so the only therapist I've ever consulted assured me, in the hope of earning praise from my mother – were used as an excuse for a trip to a Gilbert and Sullivan musical, or tea at the Savoy tearooms, twin pinnacles of Dunedin sophistication. I assume my fairy godmothers knew how complete was my mother's silence on the subject of school prizes and were quietly making amends, though, confusingly, there were brief periods when my mother showed signs of ambition on my behalf, urging me to study harder, waking me at 5 am not to clean the house but to prepare for exams.

As for birthdays, the only ones that were celebrated as a matter of course in our house were my father's and my brother's. But, again thanks to the godmothers, presents still came my way each birthday despite the lack of celebration. The one time my mother allowed me to have a party – we'd just moved to 234 – it ended in disaster. I don't remember what caused her sudden fit of rage but, with the birthday tea still uneaten, the five children I'd been allowed to invite were sent home and I was banished to my room.

*****

The first woman on whom I bestowed the title 'fairy godmother' was Auntie Grace, pretty wife of handsome Uncle Jim. I have only vague memories of the original Gladsmuir, which John and I passed on our way across the paddocks from Lauriston to school, but I can see every room of the second Gladsmuir, connected to 234 by what was to me a 'secret' gate, tucked into a hedge behind the main glasshouse. I never saw my mother go through that gate. I never saw her sit in Auntie Grace's kitchen, with its three-dimensional model of Winston Churchill, complete with cigar, in pride of place on the wall. I was the one who got to sit there, eating scones (one thinly buttered half per person – Auntie Grace didn't believe in excess), pouring out my troubles, listening to her quiet voice as she sought to distract me with stories of her own. After Uncle Jim died Auntie Grace, who had always looked delicate alongside the larger-boned Somervilles, seemed to become even smaller. 'A puff of wind would blow her away.' Whoever said that in my hearing caught exactly the anxiety I felt whenever I was with her. What if she were to vanish, as both my father and Uncle Jim had done? But Auntie Grace lived on well past my own departure from 234. A loved and loving aunt, whose gentle mockery of my mother opened up the possibility of a life lived free of the obsessive need to please.

*****

Second on my list of fairy godmothers is 'Auntie' Connie, who lived with 'Auntie' Joan, also a nurse. Were these two putative aunties lovers? It's the kind of question we ask nowadays but would never have thought to ask back then.

In the wake of the departure of Moira and Catherine, Auntie Connie's English nieces, I would occasionally be gathered up and taken for the weekend to 'The Tending House', the Broad Bay crib the two nurses owned. With predictable regularity I would fall sick, and one or other of them would tuck me up in bed, and bring me the food I loved best – Weetabix with hot milk, brown sugar and cream. Next morning, after the kind of sleep I have spent my life trying to recapture, we would go down to the bay and either swim or go out in their dinghy, idling away a Saturday as if there were no tasks to be done and no rules to be obeyed.

I don't know how many times I stayed at the The Tending House – not many, I suspect – but happy though those snatched days were, they were nothing compared to the week I spent with Connie and Joan at Lake Hawea. I must have been ten or eleven so it was about the time my mother became seriously ill. Perhaps that's why I was allowed to go. If my mother had known what I would see and hear in that glorious week of escape and adventure she would surely have forbidden me to get in the car with them. Connie and Joan may have been her friends, but I doubt she had ever seen them smoking and drinking beer, and I'm certain she'd never heard them swear.

I was to join them at their regular camping site on the shores of the lake. That in itself was enough to guarantee my excitement. Lying in my sleeping bag next to a gently snoring Auntie Connie, I imagined myself an explorer in Africa, facing dangers on a daily basis, ready to save my fellow campers from tigers and Nazis and roaring rivers. So when Auntie Joan asked me if I wanted to swim the Clutha River with her I had to say yes, even though the sight of that raging current had always terrified me. I was not a sporty child – my skill at tennis was an aberration – but I was a strong swimmer, something I presume Auntie Joan knew.

The day of the swim I was so nervous I had to keep going to the makeshift dunny concealed among the manuka further up the bank. The crossing place was some distance away from our camp so we were going to have to drive there. I can't be sure now, but I think where we ended up was a tributary of the Clutha and not the river itself, but the water still looked angry to me, the shore on the other side a vast distance away. To my amazement a small crowd had gathered. When I asked Auntie Joan why they were there she told me the swim was an annual event. People came every year to watch. 'We won't be the only ones in the water,' she informed me. 'But don't let that bother you. Just stay close to me, and ignore everyone else.'

The next thing I remember is emerging, two hours later, on the other side. I remember nothing of the swim itself. In the course of the crossing we had travelled quite a distance downstream, but try as I might I can't recreate any of it. But I can still feel the ecstasy that gripped me like a fever as a towel was wrapped around my shoulders, and Auntie Joan, running her fingers through her short-cropped hair, beamed at me and said, 'Well done, girl. You're a champion.'

*****

As a child of elderly parents I never knew what it was to have grandparents, but I did have a granny, one I adopted (or maybe she adopted me), who was as real to me as any of the grannies I encountered in my friends' houses. 'Granny Holford', my third fairy godmother, was, like Auntie Connie and Auntie Joan, a nurse. When I knew her she was retired, but at the peak of her career she had been matron of the Dunedin Hospital. The fact that of my five fairy godmothers, three were nurses and friends of my mother's, strikes me now as significant. I never heard Connie or Joan or Granny Holford criticise my mother, yet all three rescued me at various times from her iron grip. So what was going on in their minds? And what was going on in my mother's when she agreed to let me go with them?

'Your mother suffers from a form of reverse snobbery,' Granny said to me on one of my first, unsupervised visits. 'That's why she lashes out at you. It's because of who you are.'

'I don't understand.'

'You come from good stock,' she said, confusing me even more. 'That's what she can't forgive.'

'What's good stock?'

'Never mind. Just try not to blame your mother. Can you do that for me? She can't help being the way she is.'

I was already in the habit of listening to Granny as if I were Moses hearing the voice of God on the mountaintop, so I remember that conversation, which took place in her crowded, colourful home in Dunedin. Granny lived alone but her house was the opposite of lonely: photos of people in what I thought were dress-up clothes vied for prominence on shelves and sideboards and windowsills; strange, brightly coloured pictures (Granny was born in India, a country that seemed, to my enchanted eyes, to have followed her to Dunedin) dangled from picture rails;

shawls draped over chairs and sofas persuaded me that at any moment a beautiful dark-haired woman would burst through the door, gather up one of those glittering rainbow shawls and dance her way around the room.

Beside me as I write is a small framed photo of Granny Holford as a young probationer nurse. She's beautiful, her long blonde hair (grey when I knew her, but still thick and long) caught up in her nurse's wimple. Now that I know more about the times in which she lived – she was a decade and a half older than my mother – I can make up a story in which, on hearing that the love of her life has been killed at Gallipoli, she vows never to marry but to dedicate herself to the nursing profession. But I can't see her, once she has graduated to charge nurse, shouting orders at her probationers as my mother did to me. 'Look sharp, Somerville, I will be back to inspect this room in half an hour.' Granny's voice could not have differed more from my mother's. It was like my father's – full of smiles.

I wish I had thought to ask Granny more about her life. I know nothing about her family other than that they lived in India. Somewhere along the way she'd developed a love of music, and it was this we talked about more than anything else. It was she who told me – à propos, I suspect, of my mother's mental state – about Robert Schumann's breakdown and his wife Clara's devoted care of him, and about Brahms, who loved them both and never married. From there it was only a matter of time before we began talking about love and marriage and – though the word was never uttered – sex. *Jezebel*, Granny explained, was a figment of my mother's imagination. 'It has nothing whatever to do with you, or with the woman in the Bible.'

The last time I saw Granny Holford she was living in New Plymouth. I'd gone to stay with her in the wake of a traumatic experience I'd had while visiting my mother's half-sister, Aimée. My father had died six months previously. Too young (I was fourteen) to go out to work, I had been packed off to the North Island in the summer holidays to stay with various of my mother's many siblings. I never told Granny what happened to me at Auntie Aimée's. Despite what she said about Jezebel, the word retained its power. I only had to think it to feel the blood rush to my cheeks. How could I be sure, if I told Granny what had happened, she wouldn't think I was to blame?

But I did admit one thing to Granny, and that was that I didn't like New Plymouth. I couldn't give a reason. I had no idea at the time that New Plymouth was where I was conceived, so I can only explain my unease as the result of some sort of intuition about the place and my connection to it. Granny, who I suspect did know my story, accepted what I said without demur. So we spent those warm summer days talking and reading and playing the piano, sitting out in the garden when it got too hot inside, venturing no further than the dairy at the end of the street. If I'd known I would never see Granny again I would have howled like a banshee when the moment of parting came. But as we said goodbye on the New Plymouth railway station we were full of plans for my next visit. 'Your mother will be right as rain in no time, you'll see,' Granny promised. 'Mind you write to me,' she called out as the train began to move. 'And keep practising those scales.'

Granny Holford died in March 1956. I only found out about it when my letters started coming back to me. I hadn't even known she was ill. My mother had been back in Ashburn Hall for some months prior to that time, so I can't blame her for not passing on the news to me. When, on one of my spells living in the bungalow, I brought Granny's name into the conversation, Mum looked bewildered, as if she had no idea who I was talking about.

*****

The fourth of my five fairy godmothers came into my life when I was already too old to entertain such fanciful notions. But such was Bessie Thompson's generosity of spirit, and the influence she had on me, that I see her, along with Miss Buchan, whose kindness I only discovered by chance, as one of the handful of people to whom I owe more than I could ever repay.

Bessie Thompson taught speech and drama at Columba College. A woman of formidable vocal power – she taught me all I ever needed to know about projection – she had been an actress in the West End until the outbreak of war, when her parents insisted she return to New Zealand. How, after living and working in theatrical London, she coped with life in Dunedin, teaching the stout daughters of Southland farmers how to speak the poems of Robert Browning and Matthew Arnold, I can only guess. But for me she was a messenger from another universe, the teacher I would most like to be able to sit down and talk with now. My private lessons with her were the highlight of each week. Under her guidance

I flew through the Trinity College Speech and Drama exams, finishing up with a fellowship. Little wonder that I began to dream about life as an actress, an ambition Bessie encouraged but everyone else in my life at that time saw as madness.

'The greatest thing a human soul ever does in this world is to see,' John Ruskin wrote. But after my father died I began seeing only what existed in my head. The physical world still worked its magic on me, but my grasp of reality, of the business of living, weakened to the point where I only felt 'real' when I was being someone else. Day and night I dreamed of moving audiences to tears as Cordelia, Desdemona, Juliet, taking others on a journey to hell as Lady Macbeth or Medea. Having already subjected my brother and my friends to amateur theatricals at 234, plays that I would both write and, wanabe actress that I was, star in, I went on to play Eliza in the Columba College production of *Pygmalion*, Emily in Thornton Wilder's *Our Town*, and any other part I could lay my hands on. I joined the local repertory society and the Dunedin Shakespeare Club, again playing every role I was offered. I read Stanislavsky from cover to cover, learned whole scenes from Shakespeare by heart, and, egged on by Bessie, applied for a scholarship to study at the Bristol Old Vic Theatre School.

That was when reality kicked in. My mother, while she held the purse strings, was never going to support such folly. My father had left money in trust for my brother and me, but that money could only be released with her permission. I've no doubt she would have cancelled payment of my Columba fees had she been able, but my father, anticipating perhaps, had arranged for the fees to be paid by the trustees.

So I gave up my dream of becoming an actress and agreed to go to university. What I told myself then was that I would apply for drama school when I'd finished my degree, when no one could accuse me of not having 'something solid' behind me, something I could 'fall back on'. But I didn't do any of that. I got married instead.

On my last day at school Bessie gave me a silk scarf she'd bought during her time in London. I have it still, frayed at the edges from years of wearing, but as precious now as the day she gave it to me. Bessie never married. Like Auntie Connie, she shared her life with a woman friend. The same story was told about her and Lettice, another teacher, as was told about Connie and Joan – that they lost fiancés in the Great War. Today we are more inclined to attach labels. But I'm glad, in retrospect, that I grew up seeing my fairy godmothers not as creatures of a particular sexual persuasion but as magical beings, with their own closely guarded secrets.

PART FIVE: FLIGHT

'You should live your life forward and understand in the past.'
SÖREN KIRKEGAARD

Chapter Twenty-six

'Memory likes to play hide and seek ...'
GÜNTER GRASS

My father died on 11 July 1954. The following summer I was sent to stay with a succession of my mother's relatives in the North Island. I don't remember who told me this was going to happen, or who took me to the railway station in Dunedin for the start of my journey. I only remember what I felt – flutters of excitement alternating with stomach-churning anxiety – as the train steamed away from the city, skirted the familiar harbour and puffed its way towards the hills.

Where was my brother at this time? Sixteen years old, already at boarding school, he had become a stranger to me. I know he spent one summer shooting rabbits in Central Otago. And I remember him turning up the summer I worked at the milkbar in Wanaka. But where he was while I was being passed from one North Island relative to another I've no idea. Nor can I recreate the sequence of events that led me to the farmhouse where Auntie Aimée lived in Taranaki. Did I really travel on the overnight ferry from Lyttelton to Wellington on my own? Surely I would remember if I had. I have a vague sense of meals eaten in strange houses, with my mother's dire warnings ringing in my ears of what happens when vegetables (or hands) are not washed properly. The cold mutton that looked like shoe leather; the lettuce salads that were hiding places for slugs and garden dirt; the tumblers full of unboiled, tuberculosis-infected milk. But I can't give names to the people who fed me these alarming meals, then handed me over to the next relative. That is until I arrived at Auntie Aimée's. From there on I remember everything.

Auntie Aimée was married to Uncle Robin, a farmer. All I knew about my uncle before my visit was that he was a second-generation Italian. But I knew about his children – Nesta, Lynnea and Terry. It was my mother who had told me the story. We were sitting in the window seat at 234, looking out on the goldfish pond, waiting for my father to come home. My mother was gentle that day, the depression starting to bite. 'You wonder why I worry so much about Tb,' she said, turning from the window, glancing at me a moment before turning away again. 'I know you hate drinking boiled milk but it's for your own good. Your cousin Nesta died of Tb. She was 19 years old.'

'Nesta ...' I tried the name out, found it strange. 'The girl in the photo,' I said. 'In your album.'

'Contaminated milk. That's what killed her. Such a pretty lass. So like her mother ...'

I closed my eyes. The girl in the photo was a ghost – white nightdress, white skin, large colourless eyes. The only thing that wasn't white was her hair. It was light brown and curly.

'Then Lynnea fell ill,' my mother said. 'As if poor Aimée hadn't had enough to cope with. Twelve years old. Complications after rheumatic fever. I wanted to go up and nurse her but I couldn't leave your father ...'

Lynnea ... another name to roll around on my tongue.

'She weighed next to nothing when she died.'

So where is she now, I wanted to ask? What happens to you when you die?

'But that wasn't the end of it. There was a boy. Terry. He ...' My mother shook her head, as if to cancel what she'd been planning to say.

I waited. Surely she wasn't going to stop there. I touched her sleeve. 'Did he die too?' I whispered.

She shook her head again, but this time it was because she was angry. 'Questions questions,' she snapped. Then, after another long wait, in a different voice altogether, she said, 'He died of a broken heart.'

While I tried to make sense of this – people died of broken hearts in novels, but that was usually because they couldn't be with the person they loved – I kept glancing at my mother, wondering if I dared risk another question. Was Terry in love with someone? Was that why he died?

It was many years before I discovered the truth. If my mother was right, and Terry's heart *was* broken, it wasn't because of romantic love, it was because of the love he felt for his two dead sisters. Because Terry did not die of natural causes, he committed suicide. He was seventeen years old.

*****

My arrival at the remote farmhouse where Auntie Aimée and Uncle Robin lived was low key. Another aunt, kindly Muriel, drove me from the station to the house. I was to stay three nights with Auntie Aimée then move to Auntie Muriel's house in Inglewood. Auntie Aimée, a large, plump woman who bore no resemblance to my stiff, straight-backed mother, greeted me warmly, bestowing a floury kiss on me before taking my hand and leading me to one of several collapsing cane chairs scattered about the kitchen. The one I was directed to, close to the coal range, had a cat asleep on it. Auntie Aimée scooped the animal up in her arms and tossed it out the door. 'There,' she said, scraping one hand across the other to rid herself of the cat's moulting fur, 'all warmed up for you.'

While Auntie Aimée busied herself making tea for Auntie Muriel I was told to help myself to a glass of milk, an invitation I ignored. At first my two aunts chattered away as if I wasn't in the room, but then they seemed to remember I was there and started talking about my mother, what a wonderful sister she'd been when they were growing up, giving up her schooling to stay home and look after them: what a wonderful nurse she'd been, looking after her patients as if they were family. Did I realise how lucky I was to have such a mother? The way she sacrificed herself for others was inspirational.

I've no idea what I said in response to this deluge of praise. I imagine I agreed with everything they said.

When tea had been drunk, and arrangements made for my transfer in three days' time, Auntie Muriel left and I was shown to the room where I would be sleeping. Despite the fact that it was summer, the passage leading from the fuggy kitchen felt chilly, as did my bedroom at the end of the passage. 'This was Lynnea's room,' Auntie Aimée explained. 'I've left it just as it was when she was with us.'

I squeezed my eyes shut. I was to sleep in a dead person's room! But the room didn't disappear as I'd hoped it might: it was still there when I opened my eyes. A blown-up photo of Lynnea on her pony dominated the opposite wall; her dressing gown hung from a hook behind the door; her teddy bear lay on the pillow; her slippers peeped out from under the bed. 'I've cleared the top drawer for you,' Auntie Aimée said, bustling over to the dresser, rearranging the things – Lynnea's things – scattered randomly about as if they had been in use mere seconds ago. 'Now I'll leave you to unpack.'

As soon as my aunt was gone I sat down on the bed, breathing hard in an attempt to stop my heart banging about in my chest. What if Lynnea wasn't dead at all? What if she came back as a ghost? No way was I going to touch any of her things – the brush and comb set, the paua shell full of hair clips, the box of ribbons, the silver hand mirror, the gymkhana prizes pinned to the wardrobe door … I opened my suitcase, took out my pyjamas and sponge bag, and pushed the case under the bed.

Appearing again in the kitchen I was given the job of peeling potatoes. 'Your uncle's had to go into town,' Auntie Aimée told me, 'but he should be back in time for tea.'

I was still struggling with the very dirty, very knobbly potatoes when my cousin Keith appeared at the door. Keith was older than me by several years. He didn't look like his dead sisters at all. It was as if his hair had been dipped in a different paint pot – black, not light brown, the colour of his sisters' hair. Now that I have seen the family tree I realise there were two other daughters, who didn't die, but I don't remember them being in the house. Maybe they were away, or maybe, like other people I met on that strange North Island odyssey, they are playing hide and seek in my memory.

'We won't wait for Dad,' Auntie Aimée said when the potatoes were cooked. Out of the oven came a large steak and kidney pie, covered in golden pastry, reminding me how hungry I was. I'd become used by this time to the less than pristine kitchens of my mother's relatives so I was not put off by the persistent blowflies, or the strange-smelling tin in the corner of the room that I had been told contained preserved eggs. The cat had come back and was purring loudly on top of a pile of towels on one of the chairs.

We'd only just started eating when the door opened and Uncle Robin marched into the room, tossed his hat onto a chair, and, without washing his hands, sat down next to me at the table. I don't remember what he said but I remember him staring at me. I felt like staring at him too but I'd been taught that staring was rude. He was small – the kind of man I'd describe now as wiry – and dark like Keith, with whiskers growing all over the bottom half of his face. When Auntie Aimée had dished up his pie he took the plate without saying thank you and began eating noisily. 'So this is the girl you've been talking about,' he muttered, cheeks bulging with food, gravy dribbling into the whiskers on his chin.

'That's right, dear. Alice's girl.'

'Hmmm.'

'She's here till Thursday.'

I don't remember what else was said. Not much as I recall. When the meal was over I helped Auntie Aimée with the dishes while Uncle Robin read the newspaper and smoked a cigarette. Eventually it was time for bed. I kissed my uncle and aunt goodnight and scuttled down the chilly passage to Lynnea's bedroom.

Crawling under the blankets I felt a sudden panic. What if I sleepwalked? The thought was so alarming I decided I mustn't sleep at all. I'd lie awake all night, playing games if need be to stop me from nodding off. But of course I did nod off. Next thing I knew the door was opening. It was pitch dark in the room, and silent, the kind of silence that tells you there's nothing beyond the window but paddocks full of sheep and cows.

As my eyes slowly adjusted to the darkness I saw that there were two people standing in the doorway – Uncle Robin and Keith.

'Thought you might be lonely,' Uncle Robin said, advancing towards me. 'You're a long way from home … Don't be frightened now,' he added, as Keith followed him into the room.

'What are you doing?'

'Just keeping you company.'

'I'm not lonely. I was asleep.'

'Cold at nights, isn't it? Keith, you get in the other side, warm her up a bit. I'll snuggle in here.'

'No!'

'Now now, that's not very friendly.'

'Go away, *please*.'

Keith sniggered. Having squeezed himself between the bed and the wall, he was now pulling back the blankets.

'She wants us to go away,' my uncle said as he too began to pull at the blankets. 'But where does she mean us to go? We live here.'

That was when I started screaming. I had no idea I could make so much noise. The screams just kept coming, like violent, high-pitched hiccups.

Somewhere in the middle of my screaming fit my uncle and my cousin disappeared. Did Auntie Aimée come into the room then? I don't remember. All I remember is jumping out the window. It was the first time I'd done such a thing. It would not be the last.

What happened after that is a blur. I ran. I ran till I thought my lungs would burst, across damp paddocks, stumbling over shut gates, stubbing my bare feet on hidden stones, gasping with fright as cattle loomed up at me out of the darkness. I didn't stop till I saw a light. I had no idea where I was. What if the people in the lighted farmhouse sent me back to Auntie Aimée's? What would I do then?

Whatever I said to the startled, pyjama-clad man who opened the door to me must have made sense because he let me into the house and told me to wait while he put on some clothes. I don't remember mentioning Auntie Muriel's name, but as I followed my rescuer, wearing shirt and trousers now, to his car, he said, 'It's all right, lass. You're safe now. Your aunt is a friend of ours.'

Next thing I remember is standing with bleeding feet on Auntie Muriel's doorstep. She was wearing a blue dressing gown and her hair was in curlers. I couldn't hear what my rescuer was saying to her, but when he'd finished talking she reached out a hand, and pulled me inside.

Seconds later I was sitting in yet another large kitchen with a coal range and lots of chairs, but no cat that I could see. My eyes never left Auntie Muriel. Without saying a word she heated milk, added powdered cocoa and placed the steaming mug in my hand. I drank it gratefully. When I'd finished she took my hand again and led me through to the bathroom. The bath she poured was generous, and liberally sprinkled with Dettol. 'Take your time,' she said as she turned the taps off. 'You'll feel better after a good soak.'

The room I ended up in was blissfully free of dead people's things. Auntie Muriel tucked me up, kissed me on the forehead and urged me to sleep well. Next day my suitcase turned up as if by magic.

I stayed with Auntie Muriel for almost a week. I met other cousins, had picnics, went swimming in the river. No one mentioned Uncle Robin or Auntie Aimée. At the end of that week I went to stay with Granny Holford in New Plymouth.

*****

Memory tells me that all the relatives I stayed with on that summer journey were Alleys. So does that mean my mother planned the trip, organising rail tickets and ferry crossings, deciding how long I would stay at each place? The mother I remember in the months after my father died was barely able to organise a cup of tea, let alone a complex six-week holiday, so I doubt it was her. Yet I can't help wondering why the one Alley relative I truly loved – my mother's youngest half-sister Vera, who'd twice come to take care of us at 234 – was not included on my itinerary. And I can't help wondering if my mother told her siblings about *Jezebel*, and if that explains what happened at Auntie Aimée's. She told Miss Buchan, so why not her own flesh and blood?

Years later, when I'd returned to live in New Zealand, news filtered through to me of the death of my cousin Keith. He had been found dead in his bed, 'cause of death unknown'. Another decade would pass before I learned the truth. Keith, who had married and had a family, had spent two years in prison in the 1980s for the sexual abuse of his son. His death was almost certainly suicide.

My first reaction was relief. After all these years I still carried guilt about that incident in Lynnea's bedroom. But the story didn't end there. A cousin who knew my aunt and uncle well, while not doubting my story, insisted that the marriage of Auntie Aimée and Uncle Robin was happy. 'Uncle Robin was a great practical joker,' she told me. 'So was Keith. I don't know how well you remember him, but he was terrifically handsome. Girls went wild over him.'

So now I must entertain the possibility that I was wrong about my Italian uncle and his handsome son. What happened in that haunted bedroom may have been nothing more than a practical joke.

*****

It's time to take leave of my mother. After my marriage in December 1960 I saw her only intermittently till, in 1969, I went to live permanently in England and never saw her again. There were letters: the few I received were coldly formal, and always signed 'Alley Somerville'. Most letters were from me to her, accompanied by photos of my children, which I liked to imagine propped on her bedside table where she could see them every day. But it seems my mother regarded my children as indistinguishable from me. There were no photos propped up anywhere in the bungalow. One cousin witnessed both a letter from me, and a recent photo of my son, being torn up. So I can only assume that was the fate of everything I sent her.

When I became engaged to Bruce Purchase, my second husband, my soon to be mother-in-law wrote to my mother, determined to bring about a reconciliation. Marjory Purchase was a woman of considerable power, not all of it benign. She was used to getting her own way. Despite my insistence that she was wasting her time she sat down and wrote a three-page letter, extolling my virtues and finding as many ways as she could to say how delighted she was that I was marrying her son. My mother's reply was brief. It was written on the card she must have had printed in the wake of my father's death, when she elected to call herself 'Alley', the name she'd been known by when she was a nurse. 'Alley Somerville' were the words on the front of the card. On the back were the words 'Elspeth makes me sick.'

In the years that followed that abortive attempt at reconciliation I would receive only one present from her – a size 40, second-hand corset with the words 'Best wishes from Alley Somerville' tucked into the webbing. Perhaps if I had been a size 40 instead of a 'skinnymalinks' (her word) she might have formed a higher opinion of me.

Ten years after I moved to England my mother died. When I heard the news I fell into such a pit of grief I had to leave my family for a few days and go to a friend's cottage, where I could wail without questions being asked. I had long ago been disinherited, a fact that bothered my husband far more than my (to him incomprehensible) distress. I wrote a eulogy to be read at my mother's funeral. What I wanted to remember was her courage. The saddest woman I ever knew was also the bravest.

REQUIEM FOR MY MOTHER

The day you died
I was in a house you'd never seen
And would have hated
With friends you'd have called
Pretentious, or perhaps not even that –
Irrelevant, at least to you

I listened to the St Matthew Passion
And thought of all that had and had not been,
Of what you had seen and heard that
No one, least of all a child
Should see and hear

And I thought of all the oceans
That divided us
And I knew this ending was all there was
You'd never reach out now
Or hear the music played in vain for you.

Chapter Twenty-seven

'What we cannot speak about we must pass over in silence.'
WITTGENSTEIN

My father. By the standards of today he would be dismissed as an unreconstructed, patriarchal male, but since he never bullied anyone, and invariably gave orders in the form of requests, I refuse to condemn him for being unquestioningly a man of his time. Yes, he had feet of clay, he was no saint. But what people remembered about him, what they spoke of at his funeral, were the qualities he displayed every day – warmth, humour, generosity.

So far as I am aware my father was universally loved. I have only to read his obituaries to have that verified. His siblings loved him; his tribe of nieces and nephews loved him; the men and women who worked for him loved him; his fellow directors and church workers loved him; the Prime Minister and the Leader of the Opposition, both of whom sent telegrams when he died, expressed, if not love, then affection and respect. The only thing that doesn't quite fit is how he managed, in the midst of all this good feeling, to be so successful in business. But perhaps that says more about the world we live in now – when business, as often as not, is conducted on the basis of win at all costs – than it does about my father and his professional life.

When the Coull's Somerville Wilkie factory burned down – not once, but twice: the work of an arsonist with a grudge against the insurance company – my father's first concern was to reassure his employees that their jobs were secure and their wages would be paid. To the delight of my brother and me he treated the whole thing as a game, taking us on a treasure hunt to rake through the ashes. I came back the proud owner of a blackened Olivetti typewriter and a caché of singed printing equipment with which I endeavoured to construct a printing press in one of Lauriston's many sheds.

But my father did have feet of clay. 'Now I'm going to tell you a secret,' he said, coming upon me one afternoon in the toolshed at Lauriston, where I had been sent as a punishment. 'When your mother and I were on our honeymoon I broke a cup she was particularly fond of. I didn't do it deliberately. We were staying in a friend's crib near Geraldine. I was drying the dishes for her. Can't think how we came to have our wedding china with us, but we did. Your mother looked at the shattered cup on the floor, looked at me, and said, "Right Tom, that's it. You are never to set foot in my kitchen again."'

My father laughed, finishing with his characteristic snort, which always made me laugh too. He must have been wearing his business suit because I remember the fabric tickling my cheek where I had burrowed in to him, soaking up his pipe-smoky, lavender-scented smell. I was never punished when my father was around, so he must have come home early that day. 'Best thing I ever did,' he confided, kissing the top of my head. 'I was never asked to dry a dish again.'

Today that behaviour would be labelled 'learned helplessness', a quality I would confront, with none of the laughter that accompanied my father's confession, in my third marriage. Did my mother mind that the domestic burden fell so heavily on her shoulders? If she did she gave no sign of it. Not only did she wait on my father as if he were a living god, she deferred to him in all things, concealing her far more radical politics from him, so that our household struck most people who visited as a stronghold of liberal conservatism: one foot in the National Party, the other in the Presbyterian Church. Only when Uncle Rewi visited was the balance upset. Then my mother showed another face to the world. While my father muttered darkly about 'communism' and 'brainwashing', my mother rallied to her cousin's defence, warding off unfriendly journalists who showed up at the door, listening to every word Rewi had to say, as if his was the life, fighting for the poor in China, that she should have been leading, not the dreary round of domestic chores that made up her daily existence.

But Uncle Rewi only showed up once in a blue moon. The rest of the time my father held my mother's attention as light holds the attention of a moth. No luxury was too good for him. In the years when rationing books were still in use, he would be allocated twice the usual rations of cream and butter. I doubt he knew that my brother and I were missing out; he just assumed there was more than enough to go around. It never occurred to me to resent any of this special treatment, even when I looked with envy at the bath I had been instructed to run for my father, brim full of steaming hot water and lightly scented with lavender. It was just the way of things. And there were plenty of other households in Dunedin where the father was treated as a god. At least in our household the god was loved, not feared. As far as I was concerned, growing up in his shadow, he was the most important man in New Zealand, if not the world.

*****

'Never say you know the last word about any human heart.' The words were written by Henry James, a man who had no time for either biography or autobiography. My father lived for sixty-eight years before I knew him. How can I ever hope to know the truth of his 'human heart', or answer the question 'Why did he marry my mother?' But I have to try, if only to put the huge influence he has had on my life into some sort of perspective.

I had to wait till I was in my forties to get an answer, and then, in true Henry James fashion, it was only an answer of sorts. I'm back in New Zealand, recovering from a painful marriage break-up, determined to find answers to the questions about my origins that I am now asking with a sense of urgency, of time running out. I'm sitting in the living room of my cousin Jack's house in Dunedin. It's summer but the room is cold. Jack doesn't believe in 'mollycoddling'. 'If you're cold put on another jersey,' is his predictable response to requests for the heater to be turned on.

Jack and I have been talking about the family – the cousins I know personally, or have heard stories about, as well as others who are just names to me. I'm trying to get around to asking him about my parents' marriage. Last time I raised the subject I drew a blank – 'You're being ridiculous, Nookie' – so I have to come at things from a different angle.

I'm sifting through a box of old family photos. Jack is answering my questions with enthusiasm. There's nothing he likes more than identifying members of the Somerville clan and telling their stories. But he clams up when I present him with a photo of my father, aged about forty, standing, or rather leaning, with his arms around two grinning men. If it were anyone else in the photo I would say the man in the middle was drunk.

'Tell me about this one,' I say, handing the photo to Jack.

This time I will not be fobbed off. The household I was raised in was teetotal. 'Spirituous liquor', I'd been taught, was an invention of the Devil. The message was never rammed down my throat. It didn't have to be. Just knowing my father disapproved of alcohol was enough to make me view it as poison well into my adult life. So what is this photo telling me?

'Well?' I prompt.

Jack clears his throat. He too was brought up in a teetotal household, but the war has shown him a different way, and though I never saw anything approaching indulgence in his home, a whisky before dinner was commonplace, as, on celebratory occasions, was wine with the meal. 'That's your father in the middle,' Jack says. 'Not sure who the other two are.'

'What are they doing?'

'Hard to say.'

'Dad looks drunk.'

'Yes.'

'How come?'

Jack clears his throat. I can tell by the way he's moving his mouth that he is struggling, his innate honesty at war with his loyalty to my father and his reputation. Life, Jack believes, is a gift from God. It was in defence of that belief that he went to war, winning an MC for gallantry at Monte Cassino. But there can be no freedom without honesty. So what is he to do? 'You've not heard of the Somerville Curse, then,' he says.

I shake my head.

'But you have heard of Uncle Bob. Your father's brother.'

'The one no one would ever talk about? The one who drank?'

Jack nods. 'He was a farmer. A good one, from all reports. But ...'

'The curse got to him,' I provide.

'Something like that.'

'Go on.'

'After he, ah, got into difficulty, your father and my father clubbed together to support him. It went on for years.'

'Is that why my mother thought we were going to end in the poorhouse? Because the money had gone to Uncle Bob?'

'Whatever gave you that idea?'

'After Dad died it's all she talked about. I didn't even know what a poorhouse was.'

'I think that particular nightmare had more to do with your mother's life before she married,' Jack commented quietly.

'I remember Uncle Bob's wife,' I say, keen to get back to the subject of the Somerville Curse. 'Aunt Jim.'

'Aunt Jim wasn't married to Uncle Bob, she was married to Uncle John. Do try to get your facts right, Nookie.'

'Are you sure? She was scary enough to drive a man to drink! John and I were positive she was a man in disguise.'

'You and your stories.'

'Well, she did have hair growing out of her chin. And she sounded like a man, barking orders at her grown-up children as if they were still kids.'

Jack lets out a startled laugh.

'*Tea*, Catherine! Where's my tea?' I boom, in imitation. 'Why must I always be reminding you? William, the lawn needs mowing. *Now*, William, if you please!'

Jack stifles what was going to be another laugh, opting instead for a frown. 'Steady on,' he says. ('Steady on' is his default response when presented with disturbing information. Ditto 'Take it easy.' On this particular day I hear both.)

'No one ever told me her real name was Jemima,' I persevere.

'Well, I'm sorry to disappoint you but she didn't drive her husband to drink. Or her brother-in-law. Uncle Bob did that to himself.'

'With the help of the Somerville Curse … Are you telling me that's the reason my father drank too?'

'What other reason could there be?'

As I try to digest this unsatisfactory explanation, another thought occurs to me. Why, if genetics was the reason my father drank, was I never told about it? It wasn't as if I could have inherited that particular gene. What if I'd been his biological child? Would I have been told then, as a warning? 'So why the secrecy?' I ask. 'Drinking whisky isn't a crime.'

'Your father had stopped drinking long before you came on the scene,' Jack says. 'There was no need for you or your brother to be told.'

'So it was okay for me to feel guilty every time I sipped a sherry, but not for me to know the truth.'

'Now now, take it easy, Nookie. I'm sure no one set out to deliberately mislead you.'

'Then why was I told, when I married Fraser, that if I had wine at my wedding my father would turn in his grave?'

'Who told you that?'

'My mother for starters.'

'Yes, well, your mother had more than a few bees in her bonnet at the time.'

'And others in the family … Max, Tom …'

At this mention of his brothers Jack gestures impatiently. 'I know you think everything should be out in the open,' he says, 'but there's a case to be made for not parading one's failings for all the world to see. Your father's decision to become a teetotaller was both brave and wise. If, like Uncle Bob, the curse had got the better of him …' He stops, unwilling to take the thought any further.

So, I think, as the daylight slowly fades over the Otago Harbour, my father married my mother to keep him on the straight and narrow. She may have seen him as a saint, but he saw her as his saviour. What he needed was what he recognised in Alice Alley, something his devoted sister Bessie could never provide – the support of a woman who had looked into the darkness and survived.

*****

'Cut it out kiddies,' my father scolds as we drive away from Aunt Jim's house in Maori Hill. 'It's not kind to make fun of people like that.'

We're heading back to Lauriston after an agonising afternoon listening to Aunt Jim shouting orders, drinking the sickly warm milk her daughter Catherine offered us, insisting we weren't hungry when the plate of strange-shaped biscuits, with blobs of dark pink icing in the centre, was passed around. I'd whispered to John that the icing looked like blood. That was enough to ensure we both, uncharacteristically, lost our appetites.

My father's driving, erratic at the best of times, is verging on the dangerous. My brother has bet me two of his best marbles that Dad will drive over the new traffic island on Andersons Bay Road. 'Where on earth did that come from?' is his usual response to anything newfangled (and that includes traffic lights) encountered on the road. 'Wasn't there last time I looked.'

'If I tell you something,' Dad says, winking at us in the rear-vision mirror, 'you must promise never to tell anyone.'

John and I nod solemnly.

'Once, when your cousin Bill was ordered to mow the lawn – it was after he'd been in hospital and the grass had got very long – he mowed his initials, and left the rest of the lawn uncut.' My father giggles. 'What do you think of that now?'

I glance at my brother. He looks as if he's swallowed one of his precious marbles. He catches my eye and we burst out laughing.

'Not a word now,' Dad says, winking at us again. 'It's our secret.'

*****

Epilogue

Thirty years after my father's death, when I was living on my own in Stow-on-the-Wold (my daughter was at university; my son at weekly boarding school) I woke around midnight, unable to get back to sleep. I'm no believer in sudden inspiration (not without the associated perspiration), or in such tricks of the trade as automatic writing, but that night I wrote a story that seemed to write itself. I wrote all night, finishing as the church clock was striking five.

With very few changes to the text that story would prove to be my most successful, selling to a number of countries around the world. It feels right to include it here.

CHIAROSCURO

Of course she knew her father was dying. He was over seventy, and when you get ill at that age death is more or less inevitable. But the idea had no reality for her. She would come into his room the moment she got in from school and sit with him, playing cards or talking, and but for the fact that he was in bed there was nothing different about this ritual, nothing to suggest it wasn't timeless. He'd retired some years ago from his business, and though he was a busy man still – chairman of this, president of that – he was almost always there when she came home.

'Hello, Sixpence,' she'd say, bounding into the room with school bag and scarf trailing behind her. 'Hello, Tuppence,' he'd reply. 'How did it go today?' Then she'd launch into a tale of her triumphs and miseries, and he'd listen with unflagging attention, as if all the hours of her absence had been spent thinking of nothing but her.

He'd always been old, from as far back as she could remember. He was shortish, plumpish and completely bald. Her enemies at school used to tell her he wasn't her father at all, but her grandfather. She'd suffered several bloody noses on that account – wounds she was inordinately proud of later. 'If anyone says he's our grandfather again I'll kill them,' she'd boast to her brother, assuming he felt the same way. But no one ever teased him. No one would dare.

'So how did it go today?' her father asked. It was a Friday and the end, not just of the week, but of exams.

'Heaven,' she told him, dropping her bag on the floor so she could kiss him. 'Miss Johnstone told me I got top in English. And Mrs Brunton hinted I'd done really well in French.'

'That's my girl.'

'Arithmetic today. Ugh! There was a problem about the population of a town. You had to work it out from some figures you were given. I ended up with twenty-five and a half.'

'Small place.'

'I said the half was a war amputee. Do you think Mrs Miles'll be cross?'

'I don't think you'll come top.'

She grinned at him and was rewarded by a smile as dazzling as the sun. She didn't like him being in bed, or looking so thin and yellow. But she didn't mind anything else about his illness. At the weekends, when the professional nurse was off duty, she and her mother took turns to sit with him. Her mother had been a nurse before she married so she knew exactly what to do. But there was no shame or embarrassment for the girl, attending to her father's bodily needs. Feeding him the pulped food, which was all he could swallow, was a game they played. Emptying his bedpan was a source of sighs and giggles. She loved his body without thinking of it as a body. It was a seamless part of her total, trusting absorption in him.

'Do you want anything?' she asked. 'Tea? Medicine? What's in that green bottle anyway? It doesn't look like medicine.'

Her father smiled. He was a teetotaller, dying peacefully on medicinal brandy. Years later the girl would discover that her father had once been an alcoholic. The brandy that smoothed and lightened his last weeks on earth was provided by his old friend the doctor, who'd seen him through an earlier struggle and, like his daughter, loved him.

'Your mother's lying down,' he said sleepily.

The girl knelt down on the floor and opened up her scrapbook. This was her treat for finishing exams. While she sat with her father she would look back on old photos and newspaper cuttings (her father, a public figure, was often mentioned in articles), and paste in the new ones stored in a shoebox. Touching the past confirmed her belief in the future. With so much tangible evidence of her father's importance in the world, how could he be about to leave it?

Half an hour had passed when suddenly her father got an attack of the hiccups. This was a frequent occurrence but it never failed to alarm her. Sometimes it went on for an hour; once for much longer. Then she really did think he was going to die, and prayed furiously to God to stop the terrible jerking of his wasted body and make him well again.

She sat her father up and held the paper bag over his mouth, as her mother had taught her. In between spasms he grinned at her. When he could, he spoke. 'Anyone'd think I was tipsy,' he spluttered. The irony of this only struck her years later, when she began to piece together the bits of the past that weren't in the scrapbook.

At last the hiccups stopped and he fell back on the pillows. Beads of sweat clung to his forehead. They reminded her of drops of dew on a spider's web. She was afraid to touch him for fear he might disintegrate.

She wiped his face and hands, and dabbed his temple with lavender water. He was too tired even to smile now, but she didn't need that reassurance. She knew he loved her.

A few moments later he fell asleep. She pulled the covers up to his chin and kissed his glistening forehead. His face was peaceful; his breathing regular. God always heard her prayers, eventually.

As so often happened when she looked at her father, the girl felt, emanating from him, a warmth which she knew was love but which she experienced, physically, as light. In church on Sundays the minister often talked about love, comparing it to things like wind or electricity. You could see the effect, he said, but not the thing itself. But she'd never needed convincing of love's existence. From earliest childhood she'd been bathed in its light.

For several minutes the girl sat on the bed, stroking her father's hand. Her thoughts were vague and dreamy and self-centred. She saw herself famous, like her father: loved and respected for her talent. Music, writing, acting – any one could be the starting point. But mostly she saw her father's pride in her, and the joy they would both feel when she told him of her triumphs.

In the middle of this daydream her father opened his eyes, looked at her clearly and said, 'I can see Jesus.'

She was startled. It wasn't the sort of remark he made. His religion was something she saw him live, but he never talked about it. Once, in the middle of the afternoon, she found him praying. She'd burst into his bedroom and there he was, on his knees. It was the one and only time she felt guilty about him.

When he seemed to be asleep again she went back to her scrapbook.

Her mother came into the room as the light was fading. The girl looked up; smiled tentatively. Between mother and daughter there was no easy love. If it was love at all – and the girl often doubted it – it was the kind

that interferes and chastises. But today her mother was kind. She went
to the bed, leant over the sleeping figure of her husband, and came back
to ask the girl what she was doing. It was the first time she'd shown any
interest in the scrapbook.

When the girl had finished explaining her mother said, 'I'll take over
now, dear. You go and have your tea.'

She saw her mother again before she went to bed, but she didn't see her
father. 'He's resting, dear. Don't disturb him,' her mother said.

She went off to bed feeling more contented than she had in a long time.
Exams were over, and her mother had been kind. What more could she
ask?

In the night she was woken by the sound of a car pulling up outside
the house. Then she heard footsteps and, from her father's room, the
hushed, unnatural voices of visitors to the sick. She was curious to know
who'd come visiting at this hour, but not curious enough to fight off her
sleepiness.

Next morning she got up early. It was a sparkling morning, just right
for the first Saturday after exams. She was fourteen years old, and clever.
Everyone except her mother told her she was pretty. She had a best friend,
and others whom she liked a lot. If her future had been spread on the
silver grass outside her window she would have jumped right into it. Her
skin tingled with the dual excitements of achievement and anticipation.

She walked along the passage to her father's room. The door was shut.
That was unusual. She stopped and stared at the varnished wood as if
she'd never seen it before. Theirs was a Victorian house, one of the few in
town. She'd always been proud of its long, echoing corridors and its high-
ceilinged, bay-windowed rooms. You could imagine all kinds of things in a
house with so many different moods.

She looked back over her shoulder. In this passage she and her brother
played indoor hockey. 'Hockey one, hockey two, hockey three and away …!'

They could only do it when their mother was out, or when her brother had wheedled her agreement. He could wheedle just about anything out of their mother.

The house was strangely quiet. She couldn't even hear the chickens clucking. The kitchen, where her mother was sure to be, was at the other end of the passage. Perhaps she'd go there first and get a piece of toast. She'd woken hungry, though her appetite seemed now to have gone.

She pushed open the door. As she did so she was struck by the conviction that her father was dead. She drew back, terrified of what she might find. Then she made herself walk in.

The room was dark; the blinds not yet drawn. As she became accustomed to the light she saw that the bed – her father's bed – was empty.

She closed her eyes; opened them again. She hadn't imagined it. The bed was made up neatly, as if he'd never been there.

Slowly, shivering with cold, she moved across the room. She pulled the quilt off first, then the blankets, then the sheets. Not even his smell had been left behind. It was the bed of a stranger.

A few seconds later her mother came in. The girl turned to her accusingly. Later she was to remember it as a moment of pure hatred between them. The mother was always cleaning, tidying things away.

The mother spoke first. In a quiet, expressionless voice she told the girl her father had died in the night, and the undertaker had come to take the body away.

'When, when?' the girl sobbed.

'When what?'

'When did he die? Tell me!'

The mother's face crumpled and the girl felt a sudden, sickening pity for her. 'Not long after you left him,' she said. 'I saw as soon as I came in that he was near the end. I expect you were the last person he spoke to.'

The girl turned the words over in her mind, looking for the solace she sensed was there but couldn't grasp. Her mother looked terrible – wild and white, like a mountain sheep. She didn't look like the woman who'd made the bed and tidied the room and phoned for the undertaker to come.

'Why don't you come into the kitchen?' the mother said. 'I'll make you breakfast.'

Their hands met, and the girl's eyes filled with tears. She saw in that moment how it was going to be. For a few weeks, even months, she would be surrounded by hushed voices. People would treat her as a priceless object. She would be singled out, made to feel important. Then everything would go back to normal. She wouldn't be able to glory in her father's death any more. She would just be left to mourn. That would be the time (she could see it now) when she would drag herself off to a dark place – the stable loft, the bush at the back of the house, the cave on the foreshore – and howl like a wounded animal for the death of the light. The darkness would long since have closed in. From the day of his death she would have been living the life of an exile.

APPENDICES

Birth certificate pp. 204–05
Adoption documents pp. 206–17
Application seeking adoption information pp. 218–23

This is the Registrar's Certificate of Birth marked with the
letter "A" referred to in the annexed Affidavit of BETTY HILTON
JAMES made this *9th* day of *October* 1940 Before me:-
A Solicitor of the Supreme Court of New, ~~Zealand~~ NEW ZE
~~A Justice of the Peace in and for the Dominion of New Zealand~~

CERTIFIED COPY OF ENTRY IN

in the District of _____

	CHILD.				PARENTS
				FATHER.	1. When Married. 2. Where Married. 3. Previous issue of Marriage: (a) Living—Ages each (b) Dead—Number each
No.	1. When born. 2. Where born.	Christian or First Names (only).	Sex.	1. Name and Surname. 2. Rank or Profession. 3. Age. 4. Birthplace.	
(1)	(2)	(3)	(4)	(5)	(6)
	(1) *March* *5.*	*Frances*	F	(1)	(1) (2)
	(2) *...Nurs...* *...ing Home* *...te Road*			(2) (3) (4)	(3) (a) M. F. (b) M.

I HEREBY CERTIFY that the above is a true copy of an entry of birth in the Register-book kept in m

Given under my hand ____ at ____, this ____

[The fee for this certificate is 2s. 6d. for ordinary copy; 5s. for copy under seal.]

204

Year, 19⁴⁶.   [R.G.—3.

		INFORMANT.	REGISTRAR.	CHILD.
	MOTHER.	1. Signature.	1. When registered.	Name, if added or altered
xisting	1. Name and Surname. 2. Maiden Surname. 3. Age. 4. Birthplace. (7)	2. Description. 3. Residence. 4. If entry a correction of a former entry. Signatures of Witnesses attesting the same. (8)	2. Signature of Registrar. (9)	after Registration of Birth. (10)
	(1) *Betty Hilton James*	(1) *A. F. Wade*	(1) *1940 March 27.*	
	(2) —	(2) *Occupier of House.*	(2)	
	(3) *32.*	(3) *31 Wai iti Road P.W.J.*		
F.	(4) *Stratford*	(4) *Timaru Cockerill* *Deputy — Registrar.*		

ce.

f *September*, 19⁴⁶.   *(signature)* _____ Registrar.

205

IN THE MAGISTRATE'S COURT)

HOLDEN AT DUNEDIN)

IN THE MATTER of Part III of "The Infants' Act, 1908"

———— AND ————

IN THE MATTER of an Application by THOMAS SOMERVILLE and ALICE SARAH SOMERVILLE to adopt FRANCES JAMES a female child.

TO

JAMES RANKIN BARTHOLOMEW, Esquire Stipendiary Magistrate at DUNEDIN.

WE, THOMAS SOMERVILLE of Dunedin in the Provincial District of Otago and Dominion of New Zealand Company Director and ALICE SARAH SOMERVILLE wife of the said Thomas Somerville DO HEREBY APPLY to adopt as our child FRANCES JAMES a female child born at Timaru in New Zealand aforesaid on or about the Eighteenth day of March One thousand nine hundred and forty and whose mother is BETTY HILTON JAMES of Wellington in New Zealand aforesaid.

DATED at Dunedin this 30ᵗʰ day of ~~~~~ 1940.

WITNESS to the signature of)
THOMAS SOMERVILLE ~~~~~)   ~~~~~

A Justice of the Peace in and for the Dominion of New Zealand

WITNESS to the signature of ALICE)
SARAH SOMERVILLE: ~~~~~)   Alice . S Somerville

A Justice of the Peace in and for the Dominion of New Zealand

UPON READING the above Application I HEREBY APPOINT

at Dunedin aforesaid as the place and

the   day of   1940 at   as the time for

hearing the said Application.

DATED at   aforesaid this   day of

1940.

IN THE MATTER of an Application by
THOMAS SOMERVILLE and ALICE SARAH
SOMERVILLE to adopt FRANCES JAMES
a female child.

WE, THOMAS SOMERVILLE of Dunedin in the Provincial District
of Otago and Dominion of New Zealand Company Director and
ALICE SARAH SOMERVILLE wife of the said Thomas Somerville
severally make oath and say:-

1. THAT I the said Thomas Somerville am 68 years of age

2. THAT I the said Alice Sarah Somerville am 48 years of age

3. THAT we were lawfully married at Timaru in the Provincial
District of Canterbury New Zealand on the Twenty fourth day
of January One thousand nine hundred and thirty one by the
Reverend Roy Alley.

4. THAT there has been no issue of the said marriage but on
the Sixteenth day of May One thousand nine hundred and thirty
nine we adopted a male child born on the Fifth day of June
One thousand nine hundred and thirty eight and now known as
John Campbell Somerville.

5. THAT we both enjoy good health.

6. THAT we own and reside in our house and freehold property
situated at No. 50 Somerville Street Anderson's Bay Dunedin
aforesaid which we value at £2500:0:0.

7. THAT the value of our furniture therein is £500.

8. THAT I the said Thomas Somerville am Managing Director of
Coulls Somerville Wilkie Limited of Crawford Street Dunedin
aforesaid Printers and Stationers.

9. THAT the Reverend William Allen Stevely of Dunedin ..
aforesaid and Harry Renfree also of Dunedin Accountant can
speak as to our character and ability to bring up a child.

10. THAT the reason why we desire another child is because

we are both fond of children and like the company of children and furthermore we think it would be in the interests of the said John Campbell Somerville that we should adopt another child as a companion and playmate for him.

11. THAT we are well able to provide for the education maintenance and upbringing of both of the said children.

12. THAT we believe the interests of the child we now propose to adopt will be advanced by her adoption by us.

13.   THAT we are not receiving any premium for adopting the said child.

SWORN at Dunedin   aforesaid)
by the said THOMAS SOMERVILLE)
this   30th day of October   )
1940 Before me:-

A Justice of the Peace in and for the Dominion of New Zealand

SWORN at   Dunedin   aforesaid)
by the said ALICE SARAH SOMERVILLE)
this   30th day of October   )
1940 Before me:-

A Justice of the Peace in and for the Dominion of New Zealand

IN THE MATTER of Part III of "The
Infants Act, 1908"

——————   AND   ——————

IN THE MATTER of an Application by
THOMAS SOMERVILLE and ALICE SARAH
SOMERVILLE to adopt FRANCES JAMES a
female child.

I, BETTY HILTON JAMES of Wellington in the Dominion of New

Zealand Spinster one of the parents of FRANCES JAMES a female

child born on the 18th day of March 1940 HEREBY CONSENT to

an Order being made under Part III of "The Infants Act 1908"

for the adoption of the said Frances James by THOMAS

SOMERVILLE of Dunedin Company Director and ALICE SARAH

SOMERVILLE his wife.

DATED at *Wellington* this *9th* day of *October* 1940.

NESS to the signature of

TY HILTON JAMES :

B H James.

Solicitor Wellington

A Justice of the Peace in and for the Dominion of New Zealand

I, the above named BETTY HILTON JAMES mother of the said

FRANCES JAMES make oath and say:-

1. THAT the said Frances James the child who is proposed to

be adopted by the said Thomas Somerville and Alice Sarah

Somerville was born at Timaru in New Zealand aforesaid on

the 18th day of March 1940.

2. THAT hereunto annexed and marked with the letter "A"

is a Registrar's Certificate of the birth of the said Frances

James.

3. THAT no order for maintenance of the said child has been

made in any Court in New Zealand nor has any man been

adjudged the putative father of the said child.

4. THAT I well understand the nature and effect of the

foregoing Consent.

SWORN at *Wellington* this
9th day of *October* 1940
Before me:-

}

B H James.

A Justice of the Peace in and for the Dominion of New Zealand

a Solicitor of the Supreme Court of New Zealand.

I, *Winifred Fosbery Stilwell* *Wellington*
Stipendiary Magistrate HEREBY CERTIFY that the above named
BETTY HILTON JAMES appeared before me in person on the
day of *October* 1940 when I explained to her the
nature and effect of the foregoing Consent and I am satisfied
that the said Betty Hilton James thoroughly understood the
nature and effect of the said Consent.
DATED this *10* day of *October* 1940.

W F Stilwell S.M.

MEMORANDUM for :-

31st October 1940.

The Inspector of Police, DUNEDIN.

The Child Welfare Officer,
Education Department, DUNEDIN.

An application having been made by Thomas Somerville

of 50 Somerville Street, Andersons Bay Dunedin

by occupation a Company Director and his wife,

Alice Sarah Somerville for an order to adopt a

child named Frances James

and in respect of which no premium is proposed to be paid, would

you please furnish a report as early as possible on the following

points in respect of each of the applicants together with any

further particulars that can be obtained touching this matter, in

order that the Stipendiary Magistrate may be enabled to come to a

satisfactory conclusion as to whether or not it will be desirable

in the best interests of the child to grant the application.

All enquiries should, of course, be made as discreetly and

as privately as possible.

1. HABITS (as to sobriety, moral character etc.)
2. DISPOSITION (fond and kind to children or otherwise.)
3. GENERAL REPUTATION (including whether either ever convicted.)
4. Whether child, if adopted, will be well treated and cared for
   mentally, morally and physically.
5. PREMIUM How far this influences application. (Very careful
   investigation is necessary on this point.)
6. Whether adoption by applicants will be in best interests of
   the child.
7. OBJECTIONS. If there is any objection to either applicant on
   any ground whatever, please state it, however small.

4205 40

[signature] The Officer in Charge
Andersons Bay.

[signature]

[signature] Inspector
1/11/40

C. W. Carver.

Clerk of Court.

per *[signature]*

The Inspector

Please see report attached.

[signature] J.H.Brooks
Constable

NEW ZEALAND POLICE.

[Police—100A

Police-station : ANDERSONS BAY

Date : 23rd November 1940 , 19

REPORT of_____Constable J.H.Brooks_____, No. 1533

relative to Thomas Somerville and wife Alice Sarah Somerville
50 Somerville St. apply to adopt child named Frances James
Vide attached.

I respectfully report having made
discreet inquiries regarding the character and fitness
of the above named persons to adopt a child named Frances
James.

The male applicant is a well known resident of
Andersons Bay. He is a Company Director of Coull's, Somerville
Somerville, Wilkie Ltd.and is comfortable circumstances.

Mr. Somerville is a Justice of the Peace and
an ex-superintendant of the Andersons Bay Presbyterian
Sunday School, his character being beyond question.

Mrs Somerville bears an excellent character in
the district and is also a keen church woman.

Both applicants are of excellent character and
are both total abstainers from intoxicating liquor.

Both applicants are very fond of children and
their general reputation is excellent.

There is no doubt that the child if adopted
by the applicants will be well treated mentally, morally,
and physically.

No premium is being paid in respect to the
adoption.

There appears no doubt that the child if adopted
by the applicants will have an excellent home and the
adoption would be in the childs own interest.

The applicants are well known to me personally
and I consider the child will be fortunate in finding a
home where it will receive every care and attention, and
brought up in a careful manner.

Applicants have a large roomy freehold residence and
grounds and have no financial embarrassments.

Inspector of Police
DUNEDIN

The Clerk of Court,
DUNEDIN.

J.H.Brooks -

Constable 1533

Inspector of Police.

IN THE MATTER of Part III of "The
Infants' Act, 1908"

——————— AND ———————

IN THE MATTER of an Application by
THOMAS SOMERVILLE and ALICE SARAH
SOMERVILLE to adopt FRANCES JAMES
a female child.

I, WILLIAM ALLEN STEVELY of Dunedin in the Provincial

District of Otago and Dominion of New Zealand Presbyterian

Minister make oath and say:-

1. THAT I have known Thomas Somerville of Dunedin aforesaid

Company Director and his wife Alice Sarah Somerville for

ten years.

2. THAT they both are persons of good repute and fit and

proper persons to have the care and custody of the infant

child proposed to be adopted by them and of sufficient ability

to bring up maintain and educate the said child.

3. THAT I believe the welfare and interests of the said

child would be promoted by her adoption by the said Thomas

Somerville and Alice Sarah Somerville.

SWORN at Dunedin by the said   )
WILLIAM ALLEN STEVELY this 31ˢᵗ   )   W. Allen Stevely.
day of October 1940   )
Before me:-   )

A Solicitor of the Supreme Court of New Zealand

IN THE MATTER of Part III of "The
Infants' Act, 1908"

———— AND ————

IN THE MATTER of an Application by
THOMAS SOMERVILLE and ALICE SARAH
SOMERVILLE to adopt FRANCES JAMES
a female child.

I, HARRY RENFREE of Dunedin in the Provincial District of
Otago and Dominion of New Zealand Accountant make oath and
say:-

1. THAT I have known Thomas Somerville of Dunedin aforesaid
Company Director for over 30 years and Alice Sarah Somerville
his wife for over 12 years.

2. THAT they both are persons of good repute and fit and
proper persons to have the care and custody of the infant
child proposed to be adopted by them and of sufficient ability
to bring up maintain and educate the said child.

3. THAT I believe the welfare and interests of the said
child would be promoted by her adoption by the said Thomas
Somerville and Alice Sarah Somerville.

SWORN at Dunedin by the said)
HARRY RENFREE this 31ᵗʰ day)
of October 1940 Before me:-)

A Solicitor of the Supreme Court of New Zealand

214

FC/BS **EDUCATION DEPARTMENT.—CHILD WELFARE** —{C.W.—88.

Memorandum for

The Clerk of the Court,

DUNEDIN. 22nd November 1940

SUBJECT: Somerville to adopt James.

500 pads/7/37—5935l

As regards the application made by Mr and Mrs Somerville of 5 0 Somerville Street, Anderson's Bay, Dunedin, to adopt Frances James, these people are well-known citizens, in every way suitable to adopt this child. Therefore, in the circumstances, I recommend that the application of Thomas Somerville, and his wife, Alice Sarah Somerville to adopt Frances James, be approved.

Y. Clark
Child Welfare Officer.

215

THE MAGISTRATE'S COURT)
HOLDEN AT DUNEDIN   )

IN THE MATTER of Part III of "The
Infants' Act, 1908"

—————— AND ——————

IN THE MATTER of an Application by
THOMAS SOMERVILLE and ALICE SARAH
SOMERVILLE to adopt FRANCES JAMES
a female child.

W H E R E A S on the 31st day of October 1940 an Application
under Section 16 of "The Infants' Act, 1908" was duly filed in
the Magistrate's Court at Dunedin in the Provincial District
of Otago and Dominion of New Zealand by THOMAS SOMERVILLE of
Dunedin aforesaid Company Director and ALICE SARAH SOMERVILLE
his wife for an Order to adopt FRANCES JAMES A female child
born on the 18th day of March 1940 AND WHEREAS all the   ..
conditions and requirements of the said Act and the rules made
thereunder relating to the adoption of children have been duly
complied with and fulfilled and I am satisfied of the several
matters of which by the said Act I am required to be satisfied

NOW THEREFORE I, JAMES RANKIN BARTHOLOMEW Stipendiary
Magistrate DO HEREBY ORDER AND ADJUDGE that the said female
child named FRANCES JAMES may be and is hereby adopted by the
said Thomas Somerville and Alice Sarah Somerville his wife and
each of them under Section 16 of the said Act as from the date
hereof and shall henceforth bear the name of ELSPETH SANDILAND.
SOMERVILLE.

GIVEN under my hand at Dunedin
aforesaid this 5th day of December
1940.

STIPENDIARY MAGISTRATE

Birth Entry No. 103 / 1940 , of TIMARU

"FRANCES JAMES"

In pursuance of section 27 of the Births and Deaths Registration Act, 1924, I hereby notify you of an order of adoption made under Part III of the Infants Act, 1908, and of the following particulars relating thereto, viz. :—

1. CHILD :—

(a.) Full name of the child as before the making of the order :
Frances James

(b.) Date of birth of child : 18th March, 1940

(c.) Place of birth of child : Whare Nana Nursing Home, Wai-iti Road
Timaru

(d.) Sex of child : female

(e.) Full name conferred on the child by the order :
Elspeth Sandilands Somerville

2. NATURAL PARENTS OF CHILD :—

(a.) Name (or names) : Betty Hilton James

(b.) Address : Wellington

(c.) Occupation : Spinster

3. ADOPTING PARENTS :—

(a.) Names : Thomas Somerville and Alice Sarah Somerville

(b.) Address : 50 Somerville St, Andersons Bay, Dunedin

(c.) Occupation : Company Director and Wife

4. ORDER OF ADOPTION :—

(a.) Name of ~~Judge~~ Magistrate making order : J.R. Bartholomew, Esq.

(b.) Date of order : 5th December, 1940.

Dated at Dunedin

this 5th day of December , 19 40.

Clerk of Court.

(This form in duplicate to be sent to the Registrar-General, Wellington.)

IN THE DISTRICT COURT
HELD AT DUNEDIN

IN THE MATTER   of the Adoption Act 1955
                Section 23

AND

IN THE MATTER   of an application by   ELSPETH
                SOMERVILLE SANDYS   of Oxford, England
                Writer for an order that her adoption
                record be open to inspection

I, ELSPETH SOMERVILLE SANDYS of Oxford, England
Writer MAKE OATH AND SAY as follows:-

1.   THAT I am the applicant in these proceedings.

2.   THAT I am on holiday in Dunedin until the 7th day
of March 1986 when I return to England.

3.   THAT I was born at Timaru on the 18th day of
March 1940.

4.   THAT some months after my birth I was adopted
by Thomas and Alice Somerville of Andersons Bay,
Dunedin.

5.   THAT my special grounds pursuant to the
Adoption Act 1955 Section 23 (2) (c) are:-

    The desire to know my true identity has been with
me as long as I can remember. My adoptive parents were
elderly, and while I enjoyed a very loving relationship
with my father, my mother always made it plain she did not
love me and that this rejection was in some way related
to the person I was by birth.

    My adoptive father died when I was 14. My mother,
by that time, was already receiving psychiatric
treatment. Her condition deteriorated over the next
few years and she was, for long periods of time,
confined to Ashburn Hall. During these illnesses she
frequently behaved violently towards me with the result
that, for my latter teenage years, I lived with a
number of different families on a temporary basis,
returning home for only brief periods of time.

    I have an adopted brother, two years older than
me. We are fond of one another but quite unable to

218

discuss the facts of our births.

Not surprisingly, I married young. Eight years later that marriage failed. I have one daughter, twenty years old, from that marriage. She supports me whole-heartedly in my search for my birth parents.

Soon after the failure of my first marriage I married again. I realise now, 16 years later, that I married largely because I felt I had no identity of my own, and needed the framework of a marriage to "legitimise" my existence. I'm afraid I did not choose wisely, and this second marriage has since failed. I have a son, 15 from this marriage.

I have returned to New Zealand specifically to try and answer the questions that have been troubling me all my life. Unfortunately I did not realise that the law relating to Adult Adoption Information was not going to be passed until September. However, as it happens, this was the only time I could have come. My son is boarding in England for only one term and my length of stay in New Zealand is determined by that.

There are also pressing medical ███████████ reasons for my taking these steps, now, to discover my origins. ████████████████████████
████████████████████████████████
████████████████████████████████
████████████████████████████████
████████████████████████████████
████████████████████████████████
████████████████████████████████
████████████████████████████████
████████████████████████████████
████████████████████████████████
████████████████████████████████

I am not specifically seeking a relationship, or even a meeting with my natural parents, though clearly

I would be more than happy should they be alive still, and wish to meet me. What I seek is information - something to help me through my present difficulties ███████ and more generally, to dispel the ancestral darkness I have always felt surrounding me.

Although I do not have the support of my brother in this search (it is not something we can discuss), I have been lovingly supported by those members of my adoptive family to whom I am closest. My adoptive mother died in 1979.

I have for some years been a member of Jigsaw. They have helped my considerably with advice and support but have been unable, so far, to trace my birth parents.

I am fully aware of the need for tact and discretion in this matter, and agree to abide by whatever proceedings the Court recommends. One of the reasons for this application is to avail myself of the counselling and proceedural assistance as outlined in the Birthlink pamphlet, while I am in New Zealand.

SWORN at Dunedin this *16ᵗʰ*   )
day of *February* 1986)
by the said ELSPETH SOMERVILLE) *Elspeth S. Sandys*
SANDYS before me:)
)

Janet C. Somerville

A Solicitor of the High Court of New Zealand

IN THE DISTRICT COURT
HELD AT DUNEDIN

IN THE MATTER of the Adoption Act 1955
            Section 23

AND

IN THE MATTER of an application by
ELSPETH SOMERVILLE SANDYS of Oxford, England
temporarily residing in Dunedin for an order
that her adoption record be open to
inspection

The abovenamed applicant will apply to the
District Court at Dunedin on _Thurs_ day
the _6th_   day of _March_ 1986
at _3.15_   O'Cloxk in the _after_ noon
FOR AN ORDER that the Applicant's adoption
record be open to inspection pursuant to
Section 23 (2) (c) of the Adoption Act 1955
UPON THE GROUNDS set out in the Affidavit[3]
of the Applicant filed herein.

DATED at Dunedin this _17th_ day of _February_
1986

....
Solicitor for the Applicant

TO: The Registrar
        Family Court
        DUNEDIN

This application is filed by JANET
CHRISTINA SOMERVILLE whose address
for service is at the offices of Messrs
Tonkinson, Wood & Adams Bros, Solicitors
19 Bond Street, Dunedin.

IN THE DISTRICT COURT
HELD AT DUNEDIN

IN THE MATTER of the Adoption Act 1955 Section 23

AND

IN THE MATTER of an Application by ELSPETH
SOMERVILLE SANDYS of Oxford,
England temporarily residing in
Dunedin for an order that her
adoption record be open to
inspection

I, ROSALIE HEARN SOMERVILLE of Dunedin,
Community Worker make oath and say as follows:-

1. I HAVE known the applicant ELSPETH SANDYS
for almost 40 years. She is a first cousin of
my late husband the Reverend T C Somerville.

2. ON MANY occassions I visited her home when
she was a young girl.

3. THE impression I formed then, which was
confirmed in the years to follow, was that her
adoptive mother treated her very harshly. She
was often humiliated in front of visitors,
while her older brother was extolled and
praised. I have no doubt that this treatment
has left lasting scars on the sensitive
personality of this gifted woman.

4. IN LATER years, she has developed what
must be described as on obsession to discover
her true parentage. I am sure this is one of
the unsettling factors which has contributed
to the break-up of her two marriages ███████
███████████████████████████████████████.

5. SHE has never known the nurturing
influence of a "mother" and yearns for the
security that it brings. Of course it is too
late for her to experience this now, but to
know the facts about her parentage could help

her come to terms with the reality of her situation.

6.   SHE   has heard only rumours and veiled references to her parents - mostly from her adoptive mother in derogatory terms. The facts have been kept from her, which means she has an uncomfortable gap in her knowledge and understanding of herself, and therefore also of her children.

7.   I STAYED with her at her home in Oxford in 1983 and she expressed then many times her deep longing to know more of her roots. It is difficult for one who comes from known parents to understand this eroding feeling of lack of identity which arises in the mind of an adopted person, especially when relationships have gone awry with the adoptive mother.

I hope that Elspeth will have access to all the facts possible to assist her in her search for completeness.

8.   I AM willing to answer further questions on this matter that fall within my knowledge.

SWORN at Dunedin this   5ᵗʰ   day of
month   1986 before me: _Rosalie H. Somerville._

Jean A. Trunninell.

A Solicitor of the High Court of New Zealand